Herb Caen's
New Guide
to San Francisco

BY *Herb Caen*

DON'T CALL IT FRISCO

BAGHDAD: 1951

BAGHDAD-BY-THE-BAY

THE SAN FRANCISCO BOOK

HERB CAEN'S GUIDE TO SAN FRANCISCO

WITH DRAWINGS BY EARL THOLLANDER

Herb Caen's New Guide to San Francisco

AND THE BAY AREA

the Bay Bridge - Ferry Bldg. and Embarcadero

DOUBLEDAY & COMPANY, INC., GARDEN CITY, NEW YORK

Full-page illustrations courtesy *San Francisco Examiner*
Library of Congress Catalog Card Number 58–8084
Copyright © 1957, 1958 by Herb Caen
All Rights Reserved
Printed in the United States of America
Designed by Diana Klemin

Contents

7

Contents

This Is San Francisco

WILL IRWIN   "The gayest, lightest-hearted, most pleasure-loving city of the Western continent."

Welcome to one of the world's most unusual cities—a city of the world that gleams like a jewel on the western shore of America.

A compact, teeming metropolis of 800,000 people compressed into forty-four square miles at the tip of a peninsula surrounded on two sides by the greatest landlocked harbor in the world and on the third by the boundless Pacific.

In this comparatively small area, you'll find sharp reminders and soft hints of all the world's capitals. Hills like Rome. A skyscraper-studded financial district with the bustling urgency of Manhattan. A magnificent bay that ranks with Naples's and rivals the glamor of Hong Kong's. Boulevards and bistros, flower stands and winding streets, and the ever-present hint of romance and excitement that spells Paris. And the culture and tradition, plus the occasional creeping fog, of London.

San Francisco is all of these—and more. For its Old World charm is accented with the sparkle and excitement of the new. It's a city that has lived a thousand lives in its hundred years, and is still as fresh and buoyant as the ocean breezes that dance tirelessly along its hilly streets.

San Franciscans love and enjoy their city. I hope you'll enjoy finding out how and why.

How to Be a San Franciscan

ANON. "Isn't it nice that the kind of people who prefer Los Angeles to San Francisco live there?"

Having been a tourist once or twice myself, I know that no tourist likes to be taken for one. In Paris he wants to be a Frenchman, and in London he hopes to be mistaken for a Britisher. The same applies to San Francisco.

The San Franciscan is an American, speaks American, and looks more or less American, but don't be fooled. He is peculiarly San Franciscan.

He dresses in dark, generally conservative clothes. He wears a hat, even on warm days (although on *very* warm days, he might unbend to the point of carrying it in his hand). He rides cable cars on the outside step, disdaining the closed compartment even when it rains. He prefers streetcars to busses because he can run and jump onto the bottom step of a trolley, like the frustrated athlete he is. And when he drives to work, he'll park anywhere, being pretty haughty about traffic regulations.

New York impresses him, but he wouldn't dream of living there (or anywhere except San Francisco). He is scornful of Los Angeles and Oakland, and generally insular about everything beyond the Peninsula. He eats long lunches and shakes dice for the check, and reports faithfully to the nearest bar at cocktail hour, for San Franciscans, per capita, are the heaviest drinkers in the land. And perversely proud of the distinction, which has its roots in the Gold Rush days.

To him the St. Francis Hotel is the "Frantic" or "St. Foo," and the Mark Hopkins is always the "Mark," never the "Hopkins." When he talks about "the Beach," he means North Beach (the Italian section), and his fondest dream is to live on "the Hill" (which is Telegraph Hill, not Nob Hill). He lunches occasionally in the opulent Garden Court of the Palace Hotel, to remind himself of the past grandeur of his city, and although the hotel is now officially the Sheraton-Palace, having been bought by that chain, he stubbornly refuses to include the new owners. To him it was, is, and will always be the Palace, as its Bonanza King founders intended.

Although generally he can take culture or let it alone, he'll attend at least one opera during the season, as well as a symphony and even a ballet, because he was brought up to believe in these things. He likes dining occasionally in small, out-of-the-way restaurants (preferably in an alley) where he knows the waiters by their first names—and one of his great joys is "discovering" a good little restaurant his friends haven't heard of.

He is tolerant, pleasure-loving, and scrupulously careful of

Montgomery Street
San Francisco

at least two things in his speech habits. He never calls a Chinese a "Chinaman," because he knows the Chinese find that offensive, and he never *never* refers to San Francisco as "Frisco," because he considers that waterfront-born nickname beneath the city's dignity.

So if you want to be taken or mistaken for a San Franciscan, dress conservatively, cling to the outside of cable cars, ask for a dicebox after lunch, and make bad jokes about Los Angeles, even if that's your home. But don't worry about it, really. The tourist is a major San Francisco industry, and you'll be loved and pampered wherever you go and whatever you say—as long as you *don't* call it Frisco!

Before We Go On

ANON.   "Blessed are they who live by the Bay, One day they are hot, the next they are not!"

I think we should have a word about the weather in San Francisco, so that you may dress accordingly.

In a word, San Francisco's weather is unusual. *All* the time. It's rarely very hot or very cold; it's generally cool, in a somewhat unpredictable way.

A day may start out warm and balmy, and end up cold, damp, and foggy. Or the morning will begin dispiritingly with foghorns crying in the Bay, only to dissolve in a glowing swirl of mist at 11 A.M. and bright sunshine at noon. Followed again by fog at 5 P.M.

The main point to remember is that there are no seasons, as such. July and August may produce the coldest, foggiest days of the year, whereas November may bring thirty solid days of crisp sunshine. On any day of the year it is no surprise to a San Franciscan to walk along a sun-drenched downtown street and hear the foghorns blowing on the outskirts.

Furthermore, things are not even always as they seem to be. You may get a sunburn in the fog. And shiver in the sunshine. You may even be drenched by a downpour that the natives will assure you is merely "a wet fog." It hardly ever rains in San Francisco. But it wet-fogs quite a bit.

What all this adds up to, as far as you're concerned, is simply that you should bring warm clothes to San Francisco.

For a man a topcoat and woolen suits. I've never seen a man in a Palm Beach suit who didn't look as though he were shivering to death. And straw hats have a tendency to wilt in the aforementioned wet fog. As for two-tone, perforated shoes, they look a little out of place on a damp night too. Note: Most restaurants and night clubs require a necktie.

Women seem to feel most at home in San Francisco in suits. Mink coats, of course, are highly acceptable any time—and stoles come in handy too. Bring at least one pair of comfortable walking shoes, unless you're an expert at teetering up and down hilly streets on spike heels.

A word of warning: If you *insist* on wearing spike heels, be especially careful while crossing streets that contain cable-car slots. I'll never forget the day I saw a woman with her heel stuck in the slot at Powell and Sutter, with a Powell cable car bearing down on her. She waited till the final agonizing second—and then pulled her foot out of the shoe and ran for the curb. Her shoe was never the same, and neither, I fear, was she. Footnote to the shoe problem: San Francisco women rarely wear white, or "spectator," pumps.

Large hats, I've found, are more of a nuisance than they're

worth in San Francisco. I don't mean that I've ever *worn* a large hat, but I've chased plenty of them down the windy streets. They're also inclined to go shooting off your head while you're riding a cable car, making for all kinds of complications. In San Francisco the small hat is here to stay. On your head, anyway.

To sum up, you'll find San Francisco's weather generally exhilarating. And if you don't happen to like it at the moment, just wait. It'll change any second, for better or worse.

Getting Around — And How

ANON.   "Parking is such street sorrow."

There is a lot to see in San Francisco, and a lot of ways to see it. Fortunately the city covers a small area, so I think I can safely say that you can see San Francisco, in a surface sort of way, in a very few hours. It'll take you a little longer, of course, to put your finger on its elusive pulse beat, but I think you'll be able to find that, too, without the effort you might have to expend in New York. (You can search for Los Angeles's pulse beat for *years* without ever finding it. I'm not so sure it has one at all.)

If you plan to drive your own car around the city, let me start out with a few warnings.

San Francisco has a horrific traffic problem, especially in the tightly knit downtown area, where the main street, Market, slashes diagonally from the Ferry Building to Twin Peaks, making virtual dead ends of most of the other arteries.

Watch out for Market. It's a tricky devil, jammed with street-cars, busses, traffic islands, cops, and more "No Left Turn," "No Right Turn," "No—" this and "No—" that signs than you thought existed.

This traffic problem has laid a large egg called a parking problem. If you find a parking space, it's a miracle. Most of the curbs, you'll find, are painted yellow, red, green, and white, not to mention stripes, but no matter what the color, you'd better look elsewhere. San Francisco traffic cops have writer's cramp from scribbling tickets, and it could cost you anywhere from $2 to $10, not tax-deductible.

There is also a cute little tradition called the tow-away. If you park in a tow-away zone during the *verboten* hours (4 to 6 P.M.), you're likely to come back and find your car missing. It hasn't been stolen. What's happened is that a tow truck has come along and hauled your car away to a nearby (sometimes not so nearby) garage, where you will pay considerable ransom to get it back. Furthermore, if you have locked your car, you'll find that the wind wing has probably been cracked open so the tow-truck driver could get inside. Cost of repairing that is on you, too. There are large curbside signs warning you when you're in a tow-away zone. Watch for them.

Other little pitfalls you should know about include parking on hills (be sure to cramp your wheels to the curb, or it's a fat fine) and one-way streets. There are a lot of them in San Francisco, in no particular pattern, so keep your eyes peeled. There's nothing quite so disconcerting as turning a corner to find a veritable tidal wave of cars bearing down on you.

However, there are a few bright spots. Many of the downtown streets have metered zones (the meters take pennies, nickels, and dimes) where it is not impossible to find a parking place. And there are a lot of garages, some of which you may even be able to get into.

If you're *really* desperate, turn your car over to a hotel doorman, give him a four-bit tip (that's fifty cents in our parlance), and ask him to park it for you. Doormen are mysterious people who always seem to have a secret parking space up their sleeves. I mean that literally. The space *must* be up their sleeves, because I can never find one anywhere else.

Now then, just for the sake of argument, let's assume that you're behind the wheel of your car, with the engine running. You're not in a tow-away zone, you're not facing the wrong way on a one-way street, and there's no cop at your elbow, saying pleasantly, "Welcome, stranger, lemme see your driver's license."

In other words, you're ready for a tour of San Francisco—and I think I can sketch one out for you that will give you a real impression of the city in a minimum of time.

Start at the crest of Nob Hill, at the corner of California and Mason streets, where the Mark Hopkins and the Fairmont hotels and the ultra-exclusive Pacific-Union Club sit on their respective fat corners.

Before shoving off, you may want to examine for a moment "the P-U," as San Franciscans call this men's club. It occupies the tremendous brownstone mansion built in the city's Golden Age by James Flood, one of the Bonanza Kings, and it is the only one of Nob Hill's castles still in existence (its brass fence alone is worth a fortune). The P-U's few members are all righteous, Republican, and so conservative that there is some doubt whether the freewheeling Mr. Flood, were he alive today, would be admitted to membership.

Now then, on with the tour. Drive down California to Grant Avenue, turn left (past Old St. Mary's Church, over one hundred years old)—and you're in Chinatown, with its ornate lampposts, its bazaars, its tinkling Oriental sounds.

Continue to the end of Chinatown, turn right, and you will be facing Columbus Avenue, the heartbeat of the North Beach (Italian) sector. Turn left on Columbus to Lombard Street, then turn right and follow it up Telegraph Hill to Coit Memorial Tower, where you may park (if you're lucky) and drink in one of the world's great views—an overwhelming panorama of bridges, Bay, ocean, mountains, and, of course, Alcatraz, the prison island.

Coit Tower, as San Franciscans call it, is named after Lillie Hitchcock Coit, a rather eccentric but spirited young lady of an earlier era, who liked to chase fires in the company of volunteer firemen. She left part of her fortune for a "suitable memorial," and this, whether Lillie would like it or not, is it. To answer another question—no, there is no telegraph office on Telegraph Hill. In the days of the sailing ships a large wooden semaphore stood on this hill, to signal the waterfront

San Francisco's California Street

crews that a ship had entered the Bay and would soon be docking.

Leaving Coit Tower, retrace your steps down Lombard, return to Columbus, turn right on Columbus to Taylor Street, turn right on Taylor—and there you have the wonderful world of Fisherman's Wharf. Here, as in the days of yore, wriggling crabs are still boiled in huge iron containers—and it was not so long ago that a child was overheard reporting excitedly: "Gee, we had lunch at Fisherman's Wharf, and guess what—they cooked our lunch in a garbage can!"

To leave Fisherman's Wharf, drive west on Jefferson Street to Leavenworth, turn left to Bay, turn right on Bay, and continue to Van Ness Avenue. Turn left on Van Ness and you will pass the city's long Auto Row, the City Hall, the War Veterans' Memorial Building and War Memorial Opera House.

At Hayes Street turn right, then left on Gough for one block, right again on Fell Street and drive west until you reach Golden Gate Park. Continue west through Golden Gate Park to the Great Highway, which parallels the Pacific Ocean. Turn left on Great Highway and continue to Sloat Boulevard, where, on your left, you will find Fleishhacker Swimming Pool and the San Francisco Zoological Gardens.

Turning left on Sloat, drive east until you come to Portola Drive. Turn left on Portola, which will carry you past the tree-shaded mansions of St. Francis Wood and over the crest of Twin Peaks—from the top of which another magnificent panoramic view of the city will unfold (that's the teeming Mission District on the right).

Continue down Portola, which will carry you straight into Market Street. Turn left on Market (that is, if one of those ubiquitous "No Left Turn" signs isn't suddenly staring you in the face) and drive to the Ferry Building. Turn left and drive along the Embarcadero, past the row upon row of piers and the ships tugging at their lines. At this point, if you wish to return to your starting place, Nob Hill, turn left at Pacific Avenue until you reach Mason, turn left to California—and there you are, tired but bug-eyed.

This tour will take you about two hours, if traffic conditions are normal. And at the end of it you will have seen as much of San Francisco as many San Franciscans.

Cowardly footnote: The "normalcy" of San Francisco traffic conditions is open to a variety of interpretations.

If you have a little more time on your hands and care to swing through the sprawling Mission District, I recommend the 49-Mile Scenic Drive laid out by the Down Town Association. This starts at the City Hall on Van Ness Avenue, and its route is clearly marked by attractive blue-and-white signs emblazoned with a seagull. This tour *really* covers the works. Maps available through Down Town Association, 57 Post Street, DOuglas 2-7842.

Inaccurate rumors to the effect that San Francisco no longer has cable cars have floated around the world. I'm happy to say this isn't true. Yet.

There are still three cable-car lines—two running on Powell Street and one on California Street—and I can't recommend them too highly, if you're interested in the "feel" of San Francisco.

The California cable starts at the corner of California and Market streets, clatters through the financial district, climbs Nob Hill past Chinatown, the Mark Hopkins and Fairmont hotels, and comes to a rather sudden end at Van Ness Avenue. It's a good ride, but not the best buy for the money.

The two Powell Street lines cover more territory and show you more of San Francisco's many-sided charms. Both runs start on the oft-photographed wooden turntable at Powell and Market—and before you board, take a good look at the signs on the front of the cars.

The Aquatic Park-Hyde and Beach line runs up Powell to Jackson, makes a scary ninety-degree left turn—this is the famed "'Kout fer da coive!" curve—and rattles out Jackson to Hyde Street, where it turns right and takes a long, slow roller-coaster dip down Russian Hill to its turntable terminal near Aquatic Park. Among other things, you'll have a long look at Alcatraz as the car makes its groaning descent down Hyde.

However, in my opinion, the best ride is offered by the Powell cable labeled "Fisherman's Wharf-Bay and Taylor." This one also turns left at Jackson, but at Mason it swings right through parts of Chinatown and North Beach and comes to a halt at a second wooden turntable, just a short walk from Fisherman's Wharf. This is a picturesque ride, and at the end of it, you'll feel much closer to the heart of San Francisco.

All public transportation—the cables, the streetcars and the busses—is owned by the city. The fare is 15 cents, and there are almost unlimited transfer privileges.

If you have any questions, call FIllmore 6-5656 and ask for "Information." The Municipal Railway maintains a first-rate staff of question answerers, and even if you're lost in a thick fog, they can tell you in seconds how to get home.

For people who prefer to see San Francisco with a guide there's the Gray Line, which runs several different tours daily in comfortable sight-seeing busses. There is generally a man on duty at Powell and Geary, alongside Union Square, across from Hotel St. Francis. Or telephone YUkon 6-4000. Gray Line also runs a "Night Life Tour," which, for a nominal price, covers several representative night spots and will give you an impression of San Francisco's after-dark activities in a minimum of time.

The Garry Sightseeing Service (494 Geary Street, ORdway 3-7727) will provide Cadillac limousines for small groups, and a Chinatown and Night Life party for groups of twelve to fifteen.

Oh yes, the taxis. There are three principal cab companies—Yellow (TUxedo 5-1234), De Soto (ORdway 3-1414), and Luxor (ORdway 3-4040)—plus a host of smaller ones, and they all have one thing in common. The minimum charge is

50 cents. However, it's generally worth it, because San Francisco cabbies, in the opinion of seasoned travelers, are among the most courteous and helpful in the world. They can show you and tell you plenty about the city, so don't be bashful about asking questions.

If you'd like to cruise around the Bay—and don't have a friend who owns a yacht—Harbor Tours, Inc. (DOuglas 2-5414) is at your service with two sight-seeing boats that usually run four times daily—at 11 A.M., 1, 2:30, and 4 P.M.—from Pier 43 (roughly the foot of Taylor Street near Fisherman's Wharf). These tours take you as close to Alcatraz as is permissible, and you'll get a rewarding look at the San Francisco-Oakland Bay Bridge and the Golden Gate Bridge and the Marin County shore, lying north of the Golden Gate. Plus, of course, many a striking view of the city itself.

For an air tour of San Francisco and the Bay Area, Commodore Air Service runs seaplane flights daily from its base at Richardson Bay on Highway 101 just north of Sausalito, telephone EDgewater 2-1100. If you have no car, arrangements can be made to reach the base via Gray Line, YUkon 6-4000, San Francisco. Unscheduled sky tours can be arranged for four or more passengers. Commodore also runs a more or less regular flight schedule to Lake Tahoe.

Strolling and Shopping

ADMIRING VISITOR   "I love this hilly city of yours. When you get tired of walking around, you can lean against it!"

To quote an old saying I just made up, the best way to see San Francisco is by walking around. Despite the occasional steepness of the hills, there are rewards and bonuses waiting around the corner almost anywhere—in the form of unexpected views of Bay, bridges, and the city itself; in delightful old buildings and landmarks that you'd probably miss from a car or bus; and in overhearing, as you stroll, the many-tongued voices of a cosmopolitan population.

The excitement of the unexpected is everywhere in Baghdad-by-the-Bay. You may be standing on an apparently prosaic street corner on Market Street, but if you turn your eyes west, you will see Twin Peaks rearing its double-domed mass as a backdrop to the traffic plunging toward its feet.

Strolling east on Bush Street, you will be titillated by a

dramatic optical illusion—the Bay Bridge span, apparently forming a steel link between the Shell Building and the Standard Oil Building. A bridge of size, connecting the city's rival monuments to oil.

Walking along Grant Avenue in Chinatown, you may glance down an alley called Commercial Street and see, to your surprise, the Ferry Building, standing sentinel-straight on the Embarcadero. For tiny Commercial and mighty Market streets have one thing in common: they are the only streets you can look straight down—and see the Ferry Building.

And so it goes, almost anywhere you care to wander in San Francisco. Walk around that next corner and see for yourself.

UNION SQUARE AREA

If you pick this as your jumping-off place for strolling and shopping, you might start with a look around Union Square itself. ("What a town," jazzist Dizzy Gillespie once observed. "They even have a union for squares!") The origin of the name is officially unknown, but the strongest theory has it that Union supporters rallied there during the Civil War. However, the monument in the center commemorates not the victory of the North but Admiral Dewey's triumph at Manila Bay during the Spanish-American War. A San Francisco beauty of the 90's, a schoolteacher, was the model for

Looking down Commercial Street to San Francisco's Ferry Building

the bronze figure of Victory atop the ninety-seven-foot shaft
—and many an old-time San Franciscan tips his hat as he
passes the monument. Because "it is only polite to lift your
hat to your teacher." (The model for the face on the statue
was Mrs. A. de B. Spreckels, one of the city's *grandes dames*.)

Beneath the square is the four-level Union Square Garage,
and its operators modestly call it "The World's Finest Underground Garage." It holds 1700 cars. A lot—but not enough.
The garage was built to solve a traffic problem, but, as cars
wait in line to get in, it has created a traffic problem of its
own.

Strewn around the square are benches where you may
bask in the sun or huddle in the fog, as the case may be.
And strewn elsewhere are hundreds of pigeons which are re-
markably tame, endowed with excellent digestive systems,
and who cluster around your feet, cooing hopefully for a
crust of stale bread or the loan of your Diners' Club card.
Don't kick the little beggars or someone will have the S.P.C.A.
on you. In San Francisco, as in Venice, the pigeons can do
no wrong.

The city's finest shops are within walking distance of
Union Square.

At the corner of Geary and Stockton streets, and all too
visible as far as most husbands are concerned, stands I.
Magnin & Co., austere, white, magnificent, as befits the
"mother church" of this famed Coast-wide chain of women's
stores. Here you may spend 15 cents for a nail file or $1500
for a Paris creation; or you may spend $50,000 for a diamond

ring in the jewelry salon of Laykin et Cie., or you may buy nothing at all and merely use the ladies' powder room on the fifth floor, which, I am reliably informed, has gold fittings.

There are eight floors in I. Magnin's, of which the most elegant is the third. "Magnin's is so fancy," reports a seasoned observer, "that the bargain basement is on the sixth floor."

Across the street is the City of Paris department store, founded in 1850 by Felix Verdier as La Ville de Paris (he had left France because he didn't like the new Emperor). Today the store is run by his grandson, Paul Verdier, and its basement section, called Normandy Lane, is particularly interesting for its fancy foods, wines, bar, and restaurants.

Behind I. Magnin's on O'Farrell Street is the imposing home of Macy's, another of the city's first-rate department stores. This is, of course, a member of the Macy's chain. Diagonally across the street from Macy's stands Joseph Magnin, a first-rate shop for women with an excellent selection and always interesting windows (note: Joseph Magnin and I. Magnin are not related).

On the Stockton Street side of Union Square you'll find the entrance to Maiden Lane, a busy little block of intriguing shops, most noteworthy of which is V. C. Morris's china and glassware store, housed in a memorable brick structure designed by Frank Lloyd Wright. You may also enjoy browsing around the pet shop run by Ansel Robinson, and in the floral salon of Sheridan & Bell, where you will be welcomed by owner Art Bell, the "Mayor of Maiden Lane."

Warning note: You don't call it "Frisco," and you don't call Maiden Lane an "alley" without incurring the wrath of the Lane dwellers. However, if you are in a combative mood, you might remind an irate Laner that his "alley" was once Morton Street, the most notorious red-light section in the city.

The Post Street side of Union Square is lined thickly with shops. For women there are Nelly Gaffney's and John Mouber's, and for men Bullock & Jones and Robert S. Atkins. On Post between Stockton and Grant Avenue you'll find such fine women's stores as Elinor's, Ransohoff's and Carolyn Kelsey; the new (as of 1958) San Francisco home of Abercrombie & Fitch, the famed New York sporting-goods house; the imported art goods of S. Christian of Copenhagen; Shreve & Co., one of the country's fine jewelry stores; and, perhaps of the greatest interest to the sight-seer, Gump's.

Gump's, founded in 1864 by Solomon and Gustave Gump, linen merchants from Heidelberg, is perhaps most renowned for jade, but its agents have been scouring the world for decades to import all manner of rare objects. Here, in the sprawling store now guided by Richard Gump, you may buy a delicate lotus bowl from Japan for $2.50 or a pair of celadon-colored jade urns for $13,500; or, perhaps, a $3.00 ash tray from Israel, or a $16,000 necklace of perfectly matched emerald jade.

All the known colors and shades of jade are represented

In Union Square, San Francisco..

in the Jade Room of Gump's, plus a collection of tomb jade, recovered from the burial places of mandarins, that dates back two thousand years. The guest book in the Jade Room includes the signatures of Toscanini, who inscribed a bar of music from a Beethoven symphony; Schumann-Heink, Lily Langtry, Diamond Jim Brady, Sarah Bernhardt, Andrew Mellon—and yours, if you'd care to join this distinguished group.

Gump's eyes are not focused exclusively on the past, however, and you will find many examples of modern craftsmanship, plus a good representation by local artisans. There is also generally an exhibit by an outstanding contemporary artist in Gump's gallery, on the second floor.

Other shops of interest in the area:

The White House department store, at Post Street and Grant Avenue, founded in the 1850's by Raphael Weill, a daring merchant who bedazzled the early-day *nouveaux-riches* with French imports, and who was the first retailer in history to buy full-page newspaper advertisements. Among his other qualities Raphael Weill was a noted epicure, and "Chicken à la Raphael Weill" is still to be found on menus from San Francisco to Paris. The store is now run with conspicuous success by his nephew, Michel Weill. Unlike any other store I can think of, the White House closes on almost every state and national holiday of importance.

The Emporium, at 835 Market Street, San Francisco's largest department store, occupying the most highly assessed piece of land in the city. The Emporium's vast glass-domed rotunda is 110 feet around, 110 feet high.

Saks Fifth Avenue, a first-rate women's specialty shop on Grant Avenue between Post and Geary.

H. Liebes & Co., a good, medium-priced women's store, at Post and Geary.

Livingston Bros., a solid, traditional women's shop operated by the same family for three generations.

Maison Mendessolle, a specialty shop for women in Hotel St. Francis.

Robert Kirk, Ltd., at Post and Montgomery, a tasteful store for men and women, featuring, in the main, conservative British imports.

Hastings, a very complete men's store, on Post between Grant Avenue and Kearny Street (also an elegant branch in Hotel St. Francis).

Roos Bros., at Market and Stockton, a store for men, women, and children, plus an outstanding sporting-goods department.

On Sutter Street, between Powell and Mason, you'll find, among other things, the brilliant decorator's shop of Michael Taylor, in Elizabeth Arden's handsome white building. And two blocks farther down, on Sutter between Grant and Kearny, is W. & J. Sloane's, for further explorations in the field of fine furnishings.

Bookstores? Plenty of them: Books, Inc., at 336 Sutter and 156 Geary, Bonanza Inn at 663 Market, Paul Elder's at Stockton and Sutter, David Magee at 442 Post Street (second floor), Brentano's in the City of Paris (there are also large book departments in the White House, Emporium, and Macy's), Newbegin's at 358 Post, Constance Spencer at 470 Post, Tro Harper at 142 Powell, Tillman Place Bookshop, 8 Tillman Place, and John Howell's at 434 Post, the last specializing in early Californiana.

You might also get a kick out of looking in at Podesta Baldocchi, the nationally famed florists on Grant Avenue between Post and Sutter, where there is generally a spectacular display in the windows.

The largest music store in the area is Sherman and Clay, at the corner of Sutter and Kearny. And if you feel like looking at Art with a capital *A*, there's the aforementioned Gump's, the Rotunda Gallery in the City of Paris, the Maxwell Galleries at 372 Sutter, and the Oriental art objects of T. Z. Shiota at 402 Sutter and G. T. Marsh at 522 Sutter.

However, I'm not going to go into too much detail. As you stroll around this sector, you'll find shop after fascinating shop, selling all the world's goods, and all within a very few blocks of your starting place—Union Square. When you return there to rest your tired feet, remember—don't kick the pigeons! They may strike back.

Footnote to the footsore: If you come to the point where you feel you can't walk another step, hop aboard a "Shoppers' Special." These busses cover the downtown shopping area and cost only 5 cents. You can spot them by their yellow flags.

Footnote to the famished: For a quick afternoon snack, to

bolster your sagging energy and arches, ornate Blum's, on Geary next to I. Magnin's, serves snacks all afternoon, as do Townsend's at 129 Geary, Foster's at 18 Geary and 470 Sutter, Manning's at 272 Sutter and 347 Geary, Normandy Lane in the City of Paris, Goldberg-Bowen, an outstanding fancy grocery store at 242 Sutter, and Milton F. Kreis at Powell and Geary. If you're a yoghurt and blackstrap-molasses addict, there's a tiny mecca alongside Joseph Magnin's on O'Farrell near Stockton where you can give your blood sugar a shot in the arm, or whatever it needs.

CHINATOWN

The gunmen of rival tongs no longer take potshots at each other in its back alleys, the poppy perfume of opium can seldom be sniffed in its dark doorways, and the slave girls weep no more in its brothels—but for all that, San Francisco's Chinatown is still the city's most fascinating and authentic foreign colony.

(Contrary to a legend assiduously kept alive by the Chamber of Commerce, this Chinatown, with its population of about 25,000, is *not* the largest Chinese settlement outside of China; Singapore's is larger.)

Here, despite Kipling and the passing generations, East still meets West. Old ladies in pantaloons totter along on tiny feet that once were bound. In the side-street stores the merchants total your bill on an ancient abacus. In the

Chinese pawnshops the paying window is high overhead, so that the customer need not show his face (thereby "losing" it) during the transaction.

The elders still call the main street, Grant Avenue, by its original name, Dupont Gai, and to them, San Francisco is Dia Fow (Big Town) or Gum Sahn (Golden Hills). The great celebration, Chinese New Year, which starts between January 20 and February 20, depending on the full moon, is observed in all its ancient ritual for seven days and nights, punctuated with staccato bursts of firecrackers to frighten the devils away, and ending with a parade featuring a silk-and-tinsel dragon carried on the shoulders of fifty men.

Chinatown proper begins at Grant Avenue and Bush, and a walk along its eight blocks, ending at Broadway, will transport you into another world, a Cantonese-American world where the aromas and tinkly charm of the Far East mingle with the hardheadedness of the West.

You will pass shops selling teak and ivory pagodas, and shops selling television sets and multihued American sports jackets (the young Chinese of today is "sharp"). You will pass bars where the jukeboxes wail, and markets with windows that are filled with eels and octopuses, dried fish and snails, and roast ducks in golden, glazed rows. You will pass "The Culture Shop," where American comic books are sold, and vegetable stands selling long, slender string beans, peas that can be eaten pods and all, winter melons, bean sprouts, and lichee nuts. You will pass soda fountains where the kids eat "Chop Suey Sundaes," and herb stores dealing in dried sea horses, toads, snakes, and deer antlers.

Note: The names of Chinatown establishments are sometimes misleading. Do not, for example, go into the Sing Fat Co. and ask for Mr. Sing or Mr. Fat. The name means "Expanding Prosperity." Likewise there is no Mr. Wing at the Wing Sang Co.—that means "Everlasting Life." And as for the Chaan Ning Hong Co., this means "Place of Abounding Longevity."

Some Chinatown points of interest for the dogged tourist:

KONG CHOW TEMPLE, 520 Pine Street, established in 1857 by Chinese from the district of Kong Chow. Here you will find the figure of Kuan Ti, the patron deity, ruling over the seventeen other gods and goddesses of the temple.

ST. MARY'S SQUARE, on California Street near Pine, its most notable feature being Beniamino Bufano's twelve-foot granite and stainless-steel statue of Dr. Sun Yat-sen (1866–1925), father of the Chinese Republic.

OLD ST. MARY'S CHURCH, California and Grant Avenue, dedicated in 1854. The seat of Pacific-coast Roman Catholicism until St. Mary's Cathedral on Van Ness Avenue was opened in 1894, and now the parish church of the Paulist fathers. The original edifice, built largely by Chinese workmen, was partially burned in the 1906 fire-quake.

THE CHINESE CONSOLIDATED BENEVOLENT ASSOCI-
ATION, 843 Stockton, better known as the Chinese Six
Companies—although it actually includes seven "companies,"
or representatives of families from seven provinces of China.
This is Chinatown's all-powerful ruling body, settling dis-
putes, managing civic activities, etc.

OLD CHINATOWN LANE, entered via the 800 block on Washington. One of the more authentic of Chinatown's back alleys. Of especial interest is the studio of Chingwah Lee,
noted Chinese actor and scholar, whose collection of ancient
art objects is equal to that of many museums.

CHINESE TELEPHONE EXCHANGE, 743 Washington Street,
a colorful, pagoda-like structure that housed the Chinese
girls who worked as telephone operators for all of Chinatown
—and who were noted for their long memories (the older
Chinese insisted on asking for their parties by name rather
than number). For years Chinatown's exchange was, appropriately and romantically, CHina, but that, alas, has
been changed to the much less fitting YUkon 2-, and dial-
phoning is the order of the day.

BANK OF AMERICA, CHINATOWN BRANCH, 939 Grant Avenue, operated entirely by a Chinese staff, headed by Dorothy
"Dolly" Gee, an important personage indeed in Chinatown.
Here you will still find an abacus or two, for the benefit of
old customers who prefer to calculate in the ancient manner.

BUDDHA'S UNIVERSAL CHURCH, 720 Washington Street, a "do-it-yourself" structure which has been built completely by Chinese men, women, and children members of the congregation, aided by volunteers bearing such unlikely names as Spaducci, O'Leary, Gilmore, MacRitchie and Barofsky.

WAVERLY PLACE, running from Sacramento to Washington streets one-half block west of Grant Avenue, and known as "The Street of Painted Balconies." Many family associations and lodges have their ornately decorated headquarters along these two blocks. It was in a Waverly Place barbershop, incidentally, that "Little Pete," most notorious of Chinatown's hatchet men, was shot and killed by two assassins in January 1897.

SHOPPING IN CHINATOWN

So much palpable junk (a lot of it stamped "Made in Japan") is sold in Chinatown that the overly hard-eyed tourist might label the whole district a tourist trap. It isn't. Along Grant Avenue you will find some of the city's most diverting stores, operated by responsible merchants whose families have been serving the public well for generations. To name a few:

PHILIP KLEIN'S HOUSE OF JADE, 519 Grant Avenue, an interesting jewelry store where you are welcome to browse.

WA-VEL, 597 Grant, a tastefully appointed store specializing in Oriental-style shirts, dresses, robes, pajamas, etc. Quality and price high.

MADAME BUTTERFLY, 347 Grant, where you will find beautiful Chinese and Japanese silks, lounging pajamas (around $45), hand-made silk underwear.

CITY OF SHANGHAI, Grant and California. One of Chinatown's oldest stores, filled with Chinese silks and brocades, laces, kimonos, art goods, and teak furniture. Mandarin jackets from $29.50 to $750, women's evening coats from $30 to $800, Chinese table linens from $5 to $1000. If you have time, ask to see the Chinese screens upstairs. One four-paneled job of teak and solid jade is price-tagged at $25,000. Another treasure: a carved mastodon tusk valued at $50,000.

MANEON, 550 Grant, specializing in *objets d'art,* mainly porcelain and generally unusual. For example, porcelain pillows fancied by hardheaded Chinese ladies, vaselike stands for ancient mandarin hats, eighty-year-old wine jugs. These last have holes in the bottom, but somehow the wine doesn't spill out. The mystery will be explained at length.

MANDARIN FASHIONS, 512 Grant Avenue. Good assortment, good quality.

TAI PING, 701 Grant. Some good furniture, lamps, and bronze

pieces in the medium-price range. Also woven bamboo baskets from 99¢ to $10.

LUN ON, 771 Sacramento Street. Owned by the same family for fifty years, and featuring bamboo and rattan furniture and shades.

SHANGRI-LA, 667 Grant Avenue. Generally high quality; some interesting furniture in the basement.

A few additional tips to tourists: Several goldsmiths still operate in the ancient tradition along the 700 block on Jackson Street. Ah Hing, one of the last of the chair repairers (this was once a major industry in Chinatown), has his shop at 802 Stockton Street, near Sacramento. If you're after old Chinese paintbrushes and ink, they have them at House of Sung, 527 Grant. At 966 Grant there is a large grocery store called, for no apparent reason, the Italian Market; it's as completely Chinese as almost everything else in Chinatown. And at the corner of Grant Avenue and Broadway you will find, for a final fillip, a large yellow traffic sign erected by the Police Department. It's just like any other traffic sign— except that it's in Chinese.

NORTH BEACH

Where "Little China" ends, at the busy confluence of Grant Avenue, Broadway, and Columbus Avenue, "Little Italy" begins. North Beach's 70,000 citizens of Italian extraction live in a sector bounded, roughly, by Columbus on the west, Washington Street on the south, and the Bay itself on the north and east.

Like Chinatown, North Beach has a culture and atmosphere all its own. When you step across Columbus Avenue from Chinatown and enter its confines, you are stepping, in microcosm, from China to Italy. Everywhere Italian names on the shopwindows. Conversations in Italian all around you. A smell of garlic in the air—and, more often than not, the faraway strains of an accordion. Caffè espresso and cappuccino, Marca Petri and Toscani cigars, the bakeries selling panettoni, canoli, and zuppa inglese, the markets stocked heavily with zucchini, finocchio, salami, Parmesan cheese and, in the springtime, capretti (suckling kid), and the travel agencies proclaiming the wonders of a trip to the old country aboard the *Conte di Savoia* and the *Cristoforo Colombo*.

This is North Beach, which isn't a beach. Its heart is Washington Square, which isn't on Washington Street, isn't a square, and doesn't contain a statue of Washington but of Benjamin Franklin. Washington Square is bounded by

Columbus Avenue, Union, Stockton, and Filbert streets, and it nestles greenly at the feet of Sts. Peter and Paul, whose graceful twin spires make it one of the city's most beautiful churches. If you would feel the pulse of North Beach, sit for a few moments on one of the long benches in Washington Square, surrounded by the black-hatted *paesani* who lounge in the sun and reminisce about Lucca and Firenze and Roma.

North Beach leads two lives. In its back streets it is still traditionally Italian—a little world of stout mammas cooking huge and fragrant meals for their children, their cousins, and their uncles. On its main street—Broadway in the vicinity of Columbus Avenue—it is something else again: a neon-lighted madhouse of Italian restaurants, bars, and night clubs, thick with traffic from all over the city and visitors from all over the world.

For the resolute shopper there is an artsy-craftsy little section of North Beach in the 1400 block on Grant Avenue. Here, among other shops, you will find Local Color, owned by Gretchen McAllister and featuring her contemporary jewelry in silver and gold; Peter Macchiarini, who designs all kinds of jewelry in the *avant-garde* manner; and Rhoda Pack's, the oldest shop in the sector, filled with her internationally known bags, jackets, shorts in leather (she even fills orders from Paris).

As you may have heard, there is a so-called (cynics might even say "self-styled") San Francisco "renaissance" in the field of literature. The "school" includes poets Kenneth Rexroth, Lawrence Ferlinghetti, Allen Ginsberg and Gerd Stern, and novelist Jack Kerouac, and their names are spoken with a certain reverence along the bearded byways of North Beach. It was here, in such smoky caves as "The Cellar" on Green Street and "The Place" on Grant Avenue, that the fad of reading poetry to jazz backgrounds began to flourish. The closest thing to a headquarters for the cult would seem to be the City Lights Bookshop at 261 Columbus Avenue, owned by poet Ferlinghetti. He has a sizable collection of off-beat literature, with customers to match.

OTHER FOREIGN COLONIES

The Mexican colony is sandwiched in between Chinatown and North Beach, mainly along Broadway between Grant Avenue and Mason Street. Here you will find Mexican shops, bars, and restaurants—and, at 908 Broadway, Nuestra Señora de Guadalupe, the only church in San Francisco where the services are conducted in Spanish.

The Filipino colony is centered mainly along Kearny Street between Columbus Avenue and Washington Street.

The Japanese colony flourishes along Post Street in the vicinity of Buchanan Street. Of especial interest: Takahashi's at 1661 Post Street, featuring colorful imports of all kinds from Japan.

AUCTIONS, SECONDHAND STORES,

ANTIQUES

The principal auction centers are World Arts Auction Gallery (314 Sutter, YUkon 2-2359), Butterfield & Butterfield (1244 Sutter, ORdway 3-1362), and Alfred B. Clark (1185 Sutter, PRospect 6-3461). Better phone first.

There is a sometimes-fascinating collection of secondhand shops along McAllister Street, stretching roughly from the 700 to the 1000 block. Pawnshops abound along Third Street between Market and Howard.

Antique and decorators' shops are scattered all over town (on Sutter between Powell and Taylor, mainly, in the downtown area). Other larger-than-average collections are on Union Street in the vicinity of Fillmore, and Sutter Street in the vicinity of Polk Street.

If you have a deep interest in interior décor, be sure to visit Jackson Square, on Jackson Street between Montgomery and Sansome. This onetime semi-slum area has been taken over by a group of decorators and transformed into a collection of ultra-chic shops which deal exclusively with licensed interior decorators. If you have a decorator friend, you can enter these places. However, Jackson Square is rewarding, even for those who can only press their noses against the show windows.

The Restaurants

PRESIDENT WILLIAM HOWARD TAFT   "San Francisco
    knows how."

TRADER VIC   "San Francisco, the city that knows chow!"

At the moment San Francisco has about two thousand eating
places. A few of them are among the world's finest. A few
of them are probably among the world's worst. Sprinkled in
between are hundreds where you can get above-average food
at reasonable prices—for San Francisco is, and always has
been, an "eating" city, and even the lowliest cook is aware of
the tradition and strives for the specialty that will make his
greasy-spoon beanery the talk of the town.

In this respect San Francisco is a little like Paris—where,
sometimes to the surprise of strangers, food rather than sex
is Topic A. Here, as in Paris, when a stranger looks at you
across a crowded room and indicates he would whisper in
your ear, the chances are good that he doesn't want to mur-
mur words of love. He wants to confide that he's stumbled
across the most marvelous little restaurant, down a dark al-

ley, where the crab-legs meunière are done to a turn and the Montrachet is chilled exactly right.

San Franciscans started eating well in the Gold Rush days, when eggs were a dollar apiece and the first Frenchmen arrived to show the miners what to do with them. The good cooking has been predominantly French ever since, and it reached a peak in the 1890's, when such fondly remembered restaurants as the Poodle Dog, Delmonico's, the Maison Dorée, and the Maison Riche flourished.

The Italians and Chinese, too, soon made their indelible mark on the city's menus, followed by the Armenians with their kebabs and the Filipinos, who, in recent years, have developed into adept, much-sought-after cooks. These foreign influences, at work in the city's kitchens for decades, have implanted an international flavor that is here to stay. Exotic sauces and styles that would bring blank looks from the cooks and waiters in many an American city are known and understood here—in some of the smallest, unlikeliest places.

San Franciscans like to dine out. Most of the good restaurants are jammed every night—and it is fun to eat around the city, whether you're after pizza or minestrone in North Beach, a barbecued steak at Trader Vic's (the Trader is the current "king" of San Francisco cookery), or Peking duck in Chinatown. Wherever you go, you'll find yourself surrounded by other people in search of good food, and, when they find it, exclaiming over it, and enjoying it at length.

A few final words. While here, enjoy some of the specialties you'll find nowhere else—the fresh cracked crab, the tiny Bay shrimp (connoisseurs can even tell which end of the Bay they're from!), the sand dabs, the abalone. Not to mention the sour French bread and Hangtown fry (a scrambled-egg-and-oyster dish from the Gold Rush days).

In most cases it is advisable to phone for reservations. Necessary or not, it never hurts. As for tipping, there are no hard or fast rules in San Francisco. Fifteen per cent of the check should suffice. And if the waiter captain has been particularly helpful in suggesting dishes and mixing special sauces, you should tip him, say, a dollar. As for dress, neckties are required in most of the first-rate restaurants. And in a very few places—Trader Vic's, for example—small children are not particularly welcome.

Inflation being abroad in the land, I have ducked the problem of listing prices, for they seem to undergo revision almost daily—lamentably in an upward direction. And although what might seem "reasonable" to you would be "expensive" for me, or vice versa, these seem to be the only workable words at our command. Very roughly, the restaurants listed as "expensive" indicate at least $5 a person and up; "reasonable" or "moderate" means around $3 to $5; "inexpensive," a term that still applies to at least a few good restaurants, covers the $1–$3 bracket, more or less. But don't be frightened. I will always contend that you get more for your restaurant dollar in San Francisco than in any other American city.

Following is a list of San Francisco restaurants I consider above-average—if not for the food, in all cases, then for reasons of décor, price, location, or historical background. They are arranged alphabetically, not in order of personal preference. Now throw away your calorie counter, loosen your belt a notch, and go to it with both hands!

ADOLPH'S, 641 Vallejo Street, EXbrook 2-6333. Open daily except Monday from 5 P.M. to 11 P.M., Sunday from 4 P.M. to 11 P.M. Bar. This newish restaurant, in North Beach, is the kind of small place that San Franciscans love to "discover" (after which they tell their friends about it, in strictest secrecy, and the rush is on). Adolph's features a few Italian specialties, all done with loving care, and the salad plates are always carefully chilled—the mark of the above-average restaurant. Reasonable.

ALEXIS' TANGIER, 1200 California Street, TUxedo 5-6400. Open nightly except Sunday from 6 P.M. to about midnight. Alexis (last name Merab) is from the *old* Georgia by way of Shanghai, and his intimate, beautifully done restaurant is redolent of the heady atmosphere of exotic, faraway places. The bar is called the Casbah, naturally, and the cocktail waitresses float around in filmy pantaloons and sandals that turn up their noses, serving hors d'oeuvres of sou bourek (cheese puffs), piroshki (stuffed buns), and slivers of shish kebab. Alexis knows his food—and whether you want blinis with sour cream and caviar (served with iced vodka), a beautifully done rack of lamb, or lobster tails Baghdad, with mangoes, wine, ginger, and curry, you'll find the performance and the service first-rate and detailed. There is a regular dinner, but if you venture into the à la carte department, you can spend as much as the traffic (and expense account) will bear. In short, expensive.

ALFRED'S, 886 Broadway, SUtter 1-7058. Open daily from 4 P.M. to 12:30 A.M., Sundays and holidays from 2 P.M. to 12:30 A.M. If steak is your meat, Alfred's might be your place, because Mr. Bacchini (that being Alfred's last name) boasts that he is the only restaurateur on the Pacific coast who gets weekly shipments of beef from Chicago. Complete (and huge) steak dinners, and a long list of other entrees, from frog legs Florentine to sweetbreads with mushrooms. Moderate.

ALOUETTE, 1121-23 Polk Street, GRaystone 4-2166. Open nightly except Monday for dinner from 5:30 P.M. to 10:30 P.M. Bar. A quiet, pleasant French restaurant with excellent food. The coq au vin bourgignonne is especially good, and the steaks are first-rate too. Reasonable.

AMELIO'S, 1630 Powell Street, SUtter 1-9643. Open from 6 P.M. to midnight every night except holidays. The late-lamented Amelio Pacini founded this culinary landmark, and an oil portrait of him hangs in the bar, where his aging followers gather regularly to toast his memory. Meanwhile, his attractive widow, Inez, carries on in the style that made Amelio's favorably known to gourmets (and gourmands) from coast to coast. The restaurant is small, subdued, and—need I add? —expensive. For reasons unknown to me Amelio's always seems to have the sweetest, tenderest, and iciest cracked crab in town. The green noodles are superb, and the creamed spinach is just right, the steaks—especially the minute—are done to a turn, and if you still have room, try one of Amelio's specialties: asparagus della casa, a dish that contains more butter per square inch than I care to think about. Your wallet may be lighter by $10 per person by the time you leave Amelio's, but you'll be much heavier in the nicest possible way.

BARDELLI'S, 243 O'Farrell Street, YUkon 2-0243. Closed Sunday, open Monday through Friday from 11:30 A.M. to 11 P.M., Saturday from 4 P.M. to 11 P.M. A bar that is generally three deep in theatrical types, sporting figures, and assorted lawyers. Chef Charles Bardelli, a goateed Italian who was trained in France, can do fine things when the spirit moves him. For the most part, reasonable prices. Bardelli specialties: deviled breast of turkey, broiled; filet of Dover sole au vin Bardelli; squab en casserole; pancakes Jerusalem.

BERNSTEIN'S FISH GROTTO, 123 Powell Street, GArfield 1-1938. Open daily except Sunday for lunch and dinner. Bar. Bernstein's is a long way from Fisherman's Wharf, but this Powell Street landmark is more resolutely nautical than any of its Bayside rivals. Its front is decorated with a replica of the prow of Cap'n Columbus' *Santa Maria*, and village wits are fond of observing: "The way I understand it, this Bernstein started building a ship in his basement, couldn't get it out, and built a restaurant around it." In Bernstein's equally nautical but nice interior you'll find more sea food than you could possibly shake a fishing rod at, and many a non-piscatorial item, too. Moderate.

BLUE FOX, 659 Merchant Street, YUkon 6-1727. Open nightly from 6 P.M. to about midnight. Bar. Like many a great San Francisco restaurant, this one is tucked away in a dark alley which it shares with the brooding Hall of Justice and the city coroner's office. In fact the Blue Fox's slogan is "Across the Street from the Morgue"—and few phrases could tell you less about the delicacies awaiting you in this fine eating place, run with taste and distinction by Mario Mondin and Piero Fassio. Such connoisseurs as conductors Pierre Monteux and Arthur Fiedler rank this place high on their list of favorites, and their opinion is shared by thousands. There are regular dinners, but it is in the long and expensive à la carte selection that the Blue Fox shows its mettle. Mario and Piero do great things with a stuffed paste called tortellini and a unique appetizer known as veal Tonne—veal filet in a tuna sauce. Their rex sole is peerless, and the same word applies to their rack of lamb and mignonette of beef. If the sky's the limit as far as your spending goes, my advice is to let Mario do the ordering. Always bearing in mind, of course, that the jail and the morgue are only a few steps away!

BLUM'S, Polk and California streets (open daily from 8:30 A.M. to 11:45 P.M.), Geary near Stockton, next to I. Magnin's (open daily except Sunday from 9 A.M. to midnight). Other

69

branches in Fairmont Hotel, Stonestown, San Mateo, Carmel. ORdway 3-8500. A super sweetshop—no matter what the location—featuring gooey concoctions that will dismay your dentist and raise your blood sugar to dizzy heights. The Blum's shops are uniformly bright and attractive, and if you can fight your way through the quaintsy-waintsy menu ("Blumderful" is a typical coinage), you will find all sorts of calorical colossi. Ice cream, sodas, milk shakes, malts, sundaes, and parfaits without end, and a goodly array of less sugary enticements, such as pastries, sandwiches, salads, and a few entrees. The sweet tooth is generally filled, and Blum's is the same.

CANTERBURY HOTEL, 750 Sutter Street, GRaystone 4-6464. Open daily for breakfast from 7 A.M. to 11:30 A.M., for lunch from 11:30 A.M. to 2:30 P.M., for dinner from 5:30 P.M. to 9:30 P.M. Bar. The food is excellent in this well-furbished smaller hotel, a principal feature of which is an elegant landscaped garden where you may eat under colorful umbrellas —when the weather is right, of course. Tea dancing on Friday from 5 P.M. to 8 P.M., and tea every afternoon (3–5:30 P.M.) except Friday in the garden and lounge. The prices won't scare you to death, and the atmosphere is just dandy.

CHARCOAL ROOM, Drake-Wiltshire Hotel, 340 Stockton Street, GArfield 1-8011. Open daily for breakfast, lunch, and dinner. Bar adjoining. A bright, cheerful room with good food, reasonably priced. Especially popular for lunch.

CLIFF HOUSE, 1090 Point Lobos Avenue, SKyline 1-7220. Open every day for breakfast, lunch, and dinner. Bar. The fabled dining room on the edge of the Pacific, with its wide windows opening on the far horizon, and, closer at hand, the crashing surf and Seal Rocks, where countless sea lions (not seals) disport themselves most of the time (they go off to bear their young in June and July). There have been several Cliff Houses in the city's history, including a truly spectacular turreted job in the nineties, but all the predecessors have burned down. The present one is surviving nicely. Complete breakfasts—and a Sunday club breakfast from 10 A.M. to 12:30 P.M. with many choices of entree. Regular lunches from noon to 3 P.M. Reasonable.

CLIFT HOTEL REDWOOD ROOM, Clift Hotel, Geary at Taylor streets, PRospect 5-4700. Open every day for lunch and dinner. Bar. A handsome redwood-paneled room, plus an elegant adjoining room—both favored by the theatergoing crowd (the Curran and the Geary theaters are only a few steps down the street). The drinks are generous, and the food, all à la carte, is high in quality and price. Prime ribs of beef are always featured including horse-radish sauce, Yorkshire pudding, potatoes, vegetables. Baked hickory ham, with pineapple ring, sweet potato, and Cumberland sauce, is another specialty. Large salads, steaks. There are various daily specialties, variously priced, but figure around $5 a person, including drinks, to be safe.

DAVID'S DELICATESSEN, 474 Geary Street, PRospect 6-4770. Open daily except Sunday from 11:30 A.M. to about 1 A.M. People who know their kosher food make this their headquarters, and from my own sampling I'm more than willing to go along with them. The sandwiches, on rye or black Siberian soldier's bread, are of fantastic size and quality (David gets a quarter of a pound of meat into each one) and the hot dishes are "to die over," in the vernacular of its steady patrons. Prices are low—and David and his wife run most of the show by themselves. You may have to wait—but here patience is amply rewarded. First-rate all the way.

DEL VECCHIO'S, 391 Broadway, YUkon 2-3505. Open daily for lunch and dinner from 11 A.M., Sunday from 4 P.M. Bar. A solid, hardy perennial kind of North Beach institution, whose devotees have been coming back for more for years. Regular dinners with acres of hors d'oeuvres, plenty spaghet' and the usual scaloppinis, parmagianas, and marsalas. Generally reasonable.

DIMAGGIO'S, Fisherman's Wharf, ORdway 3-2266. Open daily for lunch, cocktails, dinner. Bar. Owned by the DiMaggio clan of baseball fame, of course—and Joe swings a mean neon bat tirelessly on the sign out front. He seldom drops around any more, but if you're thirsting for the sight of a real, live DiMaggio, Brother Tom is usually on hand. There's a regular dinner with such entrees as grilled rock cod, broiled salmon steak with drawn butter, veal scaloppini à la DiMaggio, and

New York steak; also a large sea-food selection, and, as befits
the DiMaggios' heritage, spaghetti, lasagne, rigatoni, mostac-
cioli, ravioli and other paste. Moderate.

DOMINO CLUB, 25 Trinity Place, EXbrook 2-5579. Open daily
except Sunday for lunch from 11:30 A.M. to 4 P.M., dinner
from 4 P.M. to midnight. Bar. The principal attraction in this
colorful spot, tucked away in an alley among the financial
district's skyscrapers, would seem to be the dozens of nude
paintings, some of them alarmingly detailed, that owner
Charlie Anderson has crammed onto his walls (his office features a photo of Sally Rand, fully dressed). If your interest
can be diverted to the menu for a moment or two, you'll find
prices in the moderate class.

EL PRADO, Plaza Hotel, Post at Stockton streets, SUtter 1-7200.
Open for lunch, cocktails, dinner. Closed Sunday. Bar. Some
of the fanciest ladies (and gentlemen) in town frequent this
favorably located, rosewood-paneled room, and when the
wind is right you can hear the buzz of conversation several
blocks away. It gets pretty frantic around cocktail hour, too.
Prices and quality high, everything à la carte. Roast beef
from the cart is a specialty which includes horse-radish sauce,
Yorkshire pudding, potatoes, vegetables. Entrees vary from
day to day. Wide variety of spectacular salads. Warning: If
you don't make a reservation for lunch, you'll wait and wait
—but then, the bar is spacious and well manned.

ERNIE'S, 847 Montgomery Street, EXbrook 2-8660. Open daily from 6 P.M. to midnight and on Sunday from 5:30 to 10:30. Bar. There is no Ernie at Ernie's—the founding father died years ago—but if he were to return, he would discover with amazement that his original small bar and eating place has grown within a very few years into one of the handsomest restaurants in this or any other city. The décor is authentically Victorian, from the downstairs bar and main dining salon to the new upstairs AMBROSIA ROOM, with its Charles Dana Gibson prints and its small mahogany bar that once graced a long-vanished San Francisco mansion. The cuisine is first-rate, in the French-Italian manner, with regular dinners and extensive à la carte selection. Fairly expensive.

EXPOSITION FISH GROTTO, 160 Jefferson Street, ORdway 3-9565. Open 24 hours a day every day with the exception of Christmas and Thanksgiving. Bar. A tremendous place that is a-crawl at all hours with crab, lobster, and assorted characters, not the least of whom is the owner, Sil Oliva, who has been in the fish business so long he is said to have developed gills. The menu is all à la carte and runs a giddy gamut from steaks, roast beef, and chicken through crab, oyster, Bay shrimps, and Louisiana prawn cocktails to rock cod cioppino with fresh crab, clams and prawns. Tucked away somewhere in this vast *salle à manger* is a coffee shop that serves breakfast at all hours. Moderate.

FAIRMONT HOTEL, California and Mason streets, DOuglas

2-8800. This busy old lady of Nob Hill has no less than five restaurants, not counting the PAPAGAYO ROOM (Mexican-American) and BLUM'S (a super ice-cream parlor), which are operated by outside interests. The pleasant CAMELLIA ROOM is open daily for lunch and dinner, all à la carte and fairly expensive. The COFFEE ROOM has a similar menu at slightly lower prices. The SQUIRE ROOM, for men only at lunch, women admitted for dinner, features steaks and salads, plus such mannish specialties as kosher frankfurters and sauerkraut and a long list of sandwiches, e.g., chopped chicken liver and corned beef, and hot pastrami. The TONGA ROOM, artfully arranged around what was once the swimming pool (there are periodic artificial thunderstorms and showers), offers a vast array of Chinese food, plus dance music. The VENETIAN ROOM, where there is dinner-dancing and "name" entertainment nightly except Monday, runs a galloping gamut from veal scaloppini to New York steak bouquetière. Yes, it's expensive.

FIOR D'ITALIA, 621 Union Street, YUkon 6-1886. Open daily from 11:30 A.M. to 1 A.M., Saturday and Sunday from 4 P.M. to 1 A.M. Bar. An old-line Italian restaurant, established in 1886, which has moved recently into handsome new quarters that embody the latest advances in restaurant design. The menu covers almost the whole range of Italian cookery—featuring a different specialty from the seven different gastronomic divisions of Italy each night, from A for Abruzzi (gnocchi with braciuoli) to P for Piemonte (polenta with chicken). Moderate.

FLEUR DE LYS, 777 Sutter Street, ORdway 3-7779. Open nightly except Sunday and Monday for dinner (kitchen closes at 10:30 P.M.). Bar. One of the finest French restaurants for miles around, rich and subdued, and presided over with consummate Gallic grace by black-bearded Robert Charles and his bubbling blond wife, Cherie. You can eat yourself into a happy stupor here on everything from escargot in mushroom heads on croutons to grenadin de veau Grand dufour to supreme de volaille Fleur de Lys—and the wine list keeps pace with the haute cuisine, to say nothing of the ambience. Those occasional low moans you will hear come from any of a number of seasoned San Francisco gourmets who make the Fleur de Lys their headquarters for gustatory reveling. The prices are no more expensive than seems fitting and proper.

FLYTRAP, 73 Sutter Street, DOuglas 2-9781. Open daily except Saturday from 11 A.M. to 9 P.M., Sundays from noon to 9 P.M. Bar. You'll find no flies in this resolutely unadorned landmark —the name goes back to its early days, circa 1895, when long strips of flypaper dangled from its ceiling—but you will find reasonable prices, huge portions, and a goodly segment of the town's financial geniuses doing business over its luncheon tables. The regular dinner features chicken, sole, or hamburger steak as entrees. Note: The Flytrap's Hangtown fry (eggs, oysters, bacon) is superb, especially if Babe—one of the owners—orders it for you. Reasonable.

San Francisco's Coit Tower - from Columbus and Union Street

FRANCISCAN, Fisherman's Wharf, near the foot of Taylor Street, DOuglas 2-7733. Open daily from 11 A.M. for lunch and dinner. Bar. A handsome new addition to the Wharf's collection of restaurants, with a terraced dining room and vast windows over the Bay, which stirs restlessly just a few feet away. All à la carte, with the usual array of fish dishes, plus steaks, roast beef, veal scaloppini, capon, etc., for those whose dish ISN'T fish. Reasonable.

GINO'S, 401 Front Street, DOuglas 2-9630. Open for lunch Monday through Friday, 11:30 A.M. to 2:30 P.M. Dinner Monday through Saturday 5 P.M. to 11 P.M. Sunday 4:30 P.M. to 11 P.M. Bar. Located near the produce district, which means you'll see at least a few characters at the bar or in the dining room. Short on décor, but long on excellently prepared food, reasonably priced. The abalone steak was great, the last time I tried it.

GRISON'S CHICKEN HOUSE, Van Ness Avenue at Pacific, TUxedo 5-2050. Not open for lunch. Dinners 4 P.M. to 9:45 P.M. Sundays 2 P.M. to 9:45 P.M. Cocktails. Consistently high quality. The menu features half chicken, chicken pot pie, prime ribs of beef, baked short ribs, trout amandine, including soup or salad, whipped potatoes, biscuits and honey, dessert, beverage. Moderate.

GRISON'S STEAK HOUSE, Van Ness Avenue at Pacific, ORdway 3-1888. Not open for lunch. Dinner 5 P.M. to 10:45 P.M.

nightly, 3 P.M. to 10:45 P.M. Sunday. Closed Tuesday. Attractive cocktail lounge with fresh-sea-food bar. Grison's is a first-rate restaurant that has maintained a consistently high standard for many years. Top-grade beef is the specialty, but the menu also includes a long list of non-beef delectables. The baked potatoes are whoppers, with cream cheese and chives, and the salads—mixed-green or coleslaw—are cold, crisp, and excellently seasoned. There are also regular dinners, which include salad or soup, entree, chili beans, potato, creamed spinach, onion rings, dessert, beverage. And a special menu for children under twelve. Mr. Grison learned the restaurant business in Europe, and he learned it well. Reasonable, considering the quality.

HANGAH TEA ROOM, 1 Pagoda Place, YUkon 2-5686. Open daily except Monday for lunch only from 11 A.M. to 3 P.M. You will find very few Caucasians in this tucked-away spot, and very few cabdrivers who can find Pagoda Place (it's off Sacramento between Grant and Stockton, and there are no pagodas whatever). Hangah features a variety of filled buns fancied by the Chinese for their long lunches, and I suggest you put yourself in the hands of a waiter. You'll get a few surprises, but they'll all be pleasant. Inexpensive.

HIPPO, 2025 Van Ness Avenue, ORdway 3-8566. Open daily from 11:30 A.M. to 2:30 A.M. (weekdays) and 3:30 A.M. (weekends) the following morning. Beer and wine only. I can't explain the name, and neither can the Hippo's owner, Jack

Falvey, who also owns a nearby liquor store called the Giraffe and a beer-and-pretzel cavern behind the Hippo called the Monkey In. Maybe he's just an anthropomorphite. At any rate, the Ivy League set monkeys around the Hippo in great numbers at all hours, wolfing down Mr. Falvey's foxy variations on the hamburger theme. Samples: Chiliburger, Tahitianburger, Swissburger, Italianburger, Scrambleburger, Russianburger, Frenchburger, Nudeburger, Curryburger and even a Bourbonburger, marinated in—oh no? Oh yes! There are other items on the menu, too, some of them equally imaginative. Moderate.

HOTEL ST. FRANCIS, Powell between Geary and Post streets, YUkon 6-2131. At the present writing the MURAL ROOM, with its rich murals, urbane waiter captains and its string quartet, is open only for luncheon—except on such special occasions as opera season. On each Monday the town's fine ladies gather in the MURAL ROOM for the "Monday lunch," a tribal ritual that started almost forty years ago and shows no signs of losing its grip. If you're in the vicinity on a Monday, poke your head in and have a look. It's quite a show. The menu is practically endless, and expensive, of course. In the same hotel there is the ENGLISH BAR AND GRILL, open for breakfast, lunch, and dinner, and featuring a first-rate bar in the old tradition, comfortable leather chairs, and high-quality, high-priced food. The nearby ST. FRANCIS TERRACE, a drinking room in the evening, is open for lunch, featuring roast beef.

HOTEL SIR FRANCIS DRAKE, Powell and Sutter streets, EX-brook 2-7755. Three attractive dining rooms in this sky-scraper hotel. The GOLDEN HIND is open daily for breakfast from 6:30 A.M., for lunch from 11:30 A.M., dinner from 5 P.M. to 9:30 P.M. Bar. Named after Sir Francis's trusty ship—but much more up to date. Club breakfasts, excellent salads (the Maurice is especially good), sandwiches, and entrees for lunch. Typical dinner entree: Javanese lamb curry with ba-nanas, rice, and Indian chutney. DRAKE'S TAVERN is open daily except Sunday for lunch and dinner. Bar. Architect Gardner Dailey designed this highly effective room in the best British manner, complete with suits of armor, battle flags that look like they accompanied William the Conqueror, and shields that many a warrior must have been borne home upon. The tavern features good old English leg of beef at lunch and prime ribs at dinner. Many entrees and excellent salads. The STARLITE ROOF is open for lunch only Monday through Satur-day. Bar. A breath-taking roof-top view of the downtown area and the Bay plus a complete smörgåsbord luncheon. Prices generally moderate.

HOUSE OF PRIME RIB, 1906 Van Ness Avenue, TUxedo 5-4605. Not open for lunch. Open nightly except Sundays and holi-days. Bar. Exclusively roast beef, served at your table from great metal carts that look like blimps. For a reasonable price you get an excellent salad, prime ribs, potatoes, creamed spinach, and beverage. Quite a bit for your money, and you'll probably have to wait for a table. The bar is to your left.

INDIA HOUSE, 629 Washington Street, EXbrook 2-0744. Closed Sunday. Bar opens daily at 5:30 P.M. Dinner served at 6 P.M. to 10:30 P.M. The lights are seductively low and the atmosphere is authentically East Indian in this excellent curry house, operated by David and Patty Brown, as attractive a couple as ever decided to turn their time and talent to the restaurant business. In the glow of candlelight turbaned Indian waiters will serve you dinner with a choice of ten curries. Or, if you prefer, Yorkshire steak and kidney pie or creamed chicken Bermuda with Dry Sack sherry. A curry dinner called Amir Ka Kahna ("Feast Fit for a King") must be ordered by noon for the same evening. While waiting at the bar try one of Mr. Brown's gimlets. He's justifiably proud of them. Reasonable.

IRON HORSE, 19 Maiden Lane, DOuglas 2-1349. Open every day except Sunday from 11:30 A.M. to 11 P.M. Much activity at the bar at noon and at cocktail hour, when hot hors d'oeuvres come around as often as the next drink. In the dining room, long list of entrees on the regular dinner, with price of entree determining cost of meal, which includes antipasto, soup, salad, dessert, beverage. Sample entrees: New York steak, prime ribs of beef, broiled half lobster. There's also a special dinner that features roast whole Cornish game hen with risotto. Large à la carte choice. And lots of decorator-type décor. Moderate.

JACK's, 615 Sacramento Street, GArfield 1-9854. Open daily except Sunday from 11:30 A.M. to 9:30 P.M., on Sunday from 4 P.M. to 9:30 P.M. Service bar. San Francisco as it was in the 1860's, brought only slightly up to date (judging from available photographs, this fine old French restaurant looks exactly as it did when it first opened its doors in 1864, except, of course, for the light fixtures; even the waiters seem not to have changed much). In the nineties, Jack's was one of the celebrated "naughty" restaurants that featured private dining rooms upstairs for the racy bird-and-bottle set—and the rooms still exist, but not for the same purpose. Today they are merely private dining rooms, no more, no less. The fine old San Francisco families still report faithfully to Jack's for dinner, and at noon the room is jammed with many of the financial district's leading citizens (notably Louis Lurie, who has lunched at his large corner table daily for some thirty years). There is a regular dinner after 5 P.M. featuring, for example, rex sole, sand dabs, leg of lamb, or boiled brisket of beef. The large à la carte menu contains such specialties as English mutton chops, roast pheasant with bread sauce, chicken Jerusalem, and roast guinea hen with orange sauce. And, of course, an endless supply of good old San Francisco sour French bread in baskets on your table. Moderate to expensive.

JULIUS' CASTLE, 302 Greenwich Street, DOuglas 2-3042. Open daily except Sunday for lunch and dinner. Bar. There is no Julius here any more (he died), but his white castle still clings to the side of Telegraph Hill, and its windows afford a fine, sweeping view of the Bay, plus a close look at life on the hill. Specialty of the house: huge banana fritters barely visible in a sea of whipped cream. Reasonable.

KAN's, 708 Grant Avenue, YUkon 2-2388. Open daily, weekdays from noon, and Saturdays and Sundays from 5 P.M. to 1 A.M. Bar. He looks young, but Johnny Kan is an old Chinatown hand with a thorough knowledge of Chinese food and Occidental tastes—and if you'll place yourself in his capable hands, he will lead you through some unusual treats. As the evening progresses, he will probably treat you to some rather bad dialect jokes, too, but stick with him. It's worth it. Kan's specialty is Peking duck (duck that has been blown up like a balloon, coated with honey sauce, roasted to a crackling turn, and served with sweet "thousand-layer" buns), but it is advisable to order this delicacy a day or two in advance. However, he does equally well with dozens of other specialties—shark-fin soup, winter-melon soup, bird's-nest soup, walnut chicken, almond duck, lobster à la Kan, chicken in parchment—everything, in fact, except chop suey, which he banned long ago (other Chinese restaurateurs soon followed suit) as an unworthy Occidental imitation. Your check at Kan's can run as high as your appetite is long, but you won't be disappointed. You might wind up the evening with an "Almond Eye," an original Kancoction in the after-dinner-drink department, and as smooth as Mr. Kan's approach.

KUO WAH CAFE, 950 Grant Avenue, YUkon 2-1851. Open daily from 10:30 A.M. to 3:30 A.M. Bar. Specialty of the house is a "tea-lunch"—very popular with the old settlers—from 10:30 A.M. to 2:30 P.M., featuring buns stuffed with spiced meats. Family-style dinners at reasonable prices. While they were in office, Harry Truman and Alben Barkley dined here several times, a fact that in no wise contributed to the later Republican victory, I am sure.

LAMBRO'S, 315 Bush Street, YUkon 6-6165. Open daily except Sunday from 11 A.M. to 11 P.M., Saturdays from 4 P.M. to 11 P.M. One of the most beautiful old bars in San Francisco—from the long-gone Waldorf Saloon on Market—graces this elegantly appointed small restaurant. Regular dinners, and a large à la carte selection, all first-rate. Reasonable.

LAMPS OF CHINA, 521 Grant Avenue, DOuglas 2-4282. Open daily except Sunday for lunch from noon to 2 P.M., for dinner from 5 P.M. to midnight. Bar. Owner George Jue has managed to cater to the tourist trade without any sacrifice of quality, with the result that his food—laboring under such precious names as "Broth of Eternal Youth," "Maiden's Prayer," and "Little Dragons on a Spree"—manages to please the visitors as well as the persnickety natives. Also steak and fried chicken, if you must. Reasonable.

LA TORRE, 375 Bush Street, SUtter 1-3119. Open nightly for dinner from 4:30 P.M., Monday through Friday for lunch from 11 A.M. Bar. One of the newer, brighter, and more successful additions to the coterie of financial-district eating places, with a long bar that seldom knows a moment of peace. A big regular dinner and extensive à la carte list, specializing in the Italian viewpoint. Prices moderate to a shade under expensive.

LE BOEUF, 545 Washington Street, GArfield 1-2914. Not open for lunch. Open every night. Bar. The name is French, but the food is good old American beef—with a gimmick. You order dinner by stepping over to a miniature butcher shop, where a butcher (union, of course) cuts a slice of steak to your specifications, slaps it on a scale, and charges you accordingly. It's served with baked potato, tossed green salad, and coffee. The prices are reasonable and I'm assuming you have a reasonable appetite.

LEOPARD CAFE, 140 Front Street, EXbrook 2-3348. Open nightly for dinner to 11 P.M., daily except Saturday and Sunday for lunch from 11 A.M. to 2:30 P.M. Bar. An attractive bustling place in the big steak, huge baked potato, crisp green salad category, with a few other entrees (sole, salmon, lamb chops) to round things out. A favored rendezvous of the pro football crowd, which is notoriously choosy about its beef. Reasonable.

LITTLE SWEDEN, 572 O'Farrell Street, GRaystone 4-9767. Open every day from 4:30 P.M. to 11 P.M. Beer and wine only. An unostentatious basement restaurant featuring a tremendous smörgåsbord. Sample entrees: surstek, flask-karre, roast Minnesota goose with red cabbage and Swedish lingenberries. Inexpensive.

LOCHINVAR ROOM, Hotel Mark Hopkins, Mason and California streets, EXbrook 2-3434. Adjoining bar. This large room, handsomely decorated in the style of Scotland as seen by Dorothy Draper, leads a long, hard, and busy life, with no signs of fatigue, from 7 A.M., when it opens for breakfast, to 1 A.M., when it closes after an evening of dancing to Bob Wellman's orchestra (nightly except Sunday). No cover charge, minimum on Saturday nights, 20% amusement tax after 8:30 P.M. Extensive dinner menu. The far-famed and highly caloric Chef's Special sandwich, on which some of the city's finest debutantes have been fattened (its most devastating ingredients are white turkey meat, creamed mushroom sauce and Parmesan cheese) is a specialty. Large luncheon menu, too, and not too frighteningly priced. All in all, a most pleasant room.

LUPO'S, 1042 Kearny Street, SUtter 1-9938. Open daily except Tuesday from 5 P.M. to midnight (sometimes later if the crowd is "good"—which it is more often than not), Sundays from 4 P.M. Beer and wine only. One of the more colorful and authentic of the North Beach pizza parlors, heavily favored by the Hollywood contingent. The owner, Papa Eduardo Cantelupo, a tenor who once sang with Caruso, is still moved to song occasionally, and his son, Frank, has been known to get down on his knees and cry in his efforts to induce you to sample a Cantelupian specialty (probably squid alla Milanaise). The prices are moderate, and if the Cantelupos find you properly receptive, you will be favored with paste or pizza in forms that defy description, because they will be improvised on the spot. Sometimes they turn out quite well, too.

NEW JOE'S, 540 Broadway, EXbrook 2-9979. Bar. Open for lunch, dinner, and on into the night until 2 or 3 A.M., depending on the size of the crowd and the whim of the bosses. This is a "character" place, and you might find a hood on one side and a socialite on the other. There are booths, but sometimes it's more fun to sit at the long counter and watch the Italian cooks in action. Joe's Special, a favorite San Francisco dish of hamburger, eggs, spinach, and onions, was invented here one late night long ago, and it's still a heavy favorite. However, you can get almost anything at Joe's—hamburgers on French bread, osso bucco (oxtails), omelets, steaks, veal Parmigiano, molto pasta. And those perennial North Beach favorites—cappuccino (a chocolate drink with milk and cream prepared under pressure, with liquor added) and caffè espresso, a high-pressure coffee with muscles. Reasonable.

NINO'S, 228 California Street, GArfield 1-3062. Open Monday through Friday at 11:30 A.M. for lunch and 5:30 P.M. for dinner, Saturday at 5:30 P.M., closed Sunday. Bar. A hideaway kind of place on the eastern fringe of the financial district, up a long flight of steps, at the top of which you'll usually find most of the town's top models and their current swains—for Nino's seems to be the place where they check their hatboxes. Co-owner Paul Pollack presides behind the bar in a sequin jacket—he has several in assorted violent shades—and the whole atmosphere is pretty clubby. The food is good and plentiful; the prices are reasonable to fairly expensive.

OLD SPAGHETTI FACTORY RESTAURANT, 478 Green Street, GArfield 1-0221. Open nightly from 5:30 P.M. to 1:45 A.M., Sunday from around noon. Beer and wines only are served over the huge old mahogany bar. This colorfully cavernous North Beach spot is indeed housed in a onetime spaghetti factory, and through the imaginative use of some of the strangest furniture this side of Early Grand Rapids, owner Fred Kuh has somehow transformed it into a kind of bewildering showplace. The food is much better than you might expect, and inexpensive, and some of the most classically bohemian types since the late Maxwell Bodenheim are constantly on view. Stare at them all you want. They'll stare right back.

OMAR KHAYYAM'S, 196 O'Farrell Street, SUtter 1-1010. Open daily from 4 P.M. to midnight, Sundays and holidays from 2 P.M. Bar. Home base of the renowned George Mardikian, who has done almost as much to reflect credit on the wide world of Armenia as William Saroyan (this was once a Saroyan hangout, incidentally). Although Mardikian is usually off on one of his diverse projects—he does everything from writing cookbooks to helping refugees to advising the Army on its mess problems—he has not allowed his restaurant to slip, and his Armenian delicacies are still as good as you'll find anywhere. Huge regular dinners featuring ajam pilaff, kouzou kzartma, Tchakhbelli chicken, or the inevitable shish kebab. Be sure to try Mardikian's sou bourek, a cheese and pastry dish. Superb! Moderate.

ORESTE'S, 118 Jones Street, GRaystone 4-5811. Open nightly except Sunday for dinner from 5:30 P.M., daily except Saturday and Sunday for lunch from 11:30 A.M. Bar. The location is a bit off the beaten path, but the Italian food is fine and mellow in this smallish restaurant run by guaranteed 100 per cent authentic Italians. Excellent paste—fettucini, baked green lasagne, cannelloni, etc.—and more entrees than you'd think Chef Oreste has room for in his confined kitchen. Prices reasonable to moderately expensive, portions huge, calories unlimited.

OWL 'N' TURTLE, 615 Washington Street, EXbrook 7-0335. Open daily for lunch and dinner, open Sunday from 3 P.M. Bar. The name derives from an owl that is standing on a turtle's back—both are bronze—and the piece is but one of many *objets d'art* and d'otherwise that distinguish this fairly new eating place (the two-headed fixture over the bar once lighted a lord's billiard table in England, for example).

Luncheon is all à la carte and widely varied; many salads, Irish stew, Spanish omelet, minute steak, abalone, calf's liver, to give you an idea. The regular dinner runs through the usual choices from Wiener Schnitzel to New York cuts. Reasonable.

PANELLI'S, 453 Pine Street, DOuglas 2-7198. Open daily from 11:30 A.M. to 1 A.M. Bar. This thriving spot, in the heart of the financial district, calls itself "The House of Conviviality," and there is, indeed, a mighty hubbub at all hours among Panelli's loyal devotees. The regular dinner offers no fewer than twenty-three choices of entree, from deep-sea bass to charcoal-broiled steaks, and the à la carte menu is equally diverse. Especially fine selection of pasta, if you're the type that can ignore the old San Francisco admonition: "Paste makes waist." Reasonable.

PAOLI'S, 347 Montgomery Street, SUtter 1-7115. Open every day from 11 A.M. to 11:30 P.M., Saturday, Sunday, and holidays from 4 P.M. to 11:30 P.M. There's a tremendous bar, which is generally hidden behind a bottle array of youngish Brooks Bros. types, with girls to match. Free hot hors d'oeuvres are passed from time to time—and *just* in time, in some cases. If you can tear yourself away from the party atmosphere, you'll find the food good and fairly reasonable. A handsome new room called the Pinafore has been added by Mr. Paoli to his always-jam-packed institution.

PAPAGAYO ROOM, Fairmont Hotel, California and Mason streets, DOuglas 2-5650. Open nightly from 5:30 P.M. to 3 A.M. Bar. A-bustling all the time, especially after midnight, when most of the town's show people congregate to trade gossip with Al Williams, the owner and a most ingratiating host who knows everybody—including, to your momentary surprise, you. Adding to the din are parrots, squawking in their cages on the walls, and a saucy white cockatoo that guards the entrance and will be happy to take a nip out of your finger. Mexican food is featured, but there is a wide range of first-rate American dishes, too—most of them pleasantly priced and all of them pleasantly served by an appetizing crew of waitresses in off-the-shoulder blouses.

PENTHOUSE BUFFETERIA, penthouse, H. Liebes & Co. (women's apparel), Geary Street and Grant Avenue. Open for lunch Monday through Saturday. A roof-top cafeteria, handy for a good quick snack in the middle of your shopping. Chuckburgers, diet plates, and a good selection of delicatessen-type sandwiches and salads. View of the downtown area. Inexpensive.

PIETRO'S, 311 Washington Street, YUkon 6-0605. Open Tuesday through Saturday for lunch, 11:30 A.M. to 2 P.M., for dinner until 10 P.M. In the heart of the produce district, with its cavernous sheds, long shadows, and leather-jacketed workers. Pietro's own crew is largely Italian, and it's a bad night indeed when one of the waiters doesn't burst into an operatic aria. If you can outsing him, go to it—Pietro will probably send you a bottle of wine. Regular luncheon includes soup or salad, entree, dessert, and coffee. Regular dinners are moderately priced—and there are various little "package" deals, such as club steak, mixed green salad, baked potato, and vegetable. If you like unusual Italian desserts, ask Pietro about Angelia Pia. And in the wine department you might enjoy his Paul Rossigneux cabernet rosé—as good a rosé as I've ever tasted.

PIRO'S, 714 Montgomery Street, YUkon 2-3921. Bar. Open for lunch daily except Saturday and Sunday from 11:30 A.M. to 2:30 P.M., open nightly for dinner from 5 to 11 P.M. Bar. Here, the décor is attractively modern, the atmosphere is burstingly gay, and there is usually a crowd waiting for tables—which tells you all you need to know about the quality of the food. Piro's makes fettucini that's every bit as good as Alfredo's in Rome, and the dinners run with the usual giddy gamut from filet of sole through veal scaloppini to chicken Jerusalem and entrecôte steak. However, Piro's à la carte menu is long on pastes, salads, and entrees, and you can keep the price just about where you want it and still dine surpassingly.

PLACE PIGALLE, 3721 Buchanan Street, WEst 1-6997. Open nightly except Monday from 6 P.M. to midnight. Bar. A French restaurant as Hollywood might imagine it, complete with strolling violinist who usually pokes his fiddle into your booth just as you're getting to the punch line of your favorite joke. Not too expensive. Complete dinners with such specialties as carre d'agneau boulangère, coq au vin, and entrecôte de boeuf rotie, chasseur. Eh bien and Mon Dieu.

RITZ OLD POODLE DOG, 65 Post Street, SUtter 1-1919. Open daily from 11:30 A.M. to 9:30 P.M., Sunday from 4 P.M. to 9:30 P.M. Bar. The Poodle Dog is one of the famous names in this city's culinary history—the first one was established in the days of '49 as, reportedly, the Poulet d'Or, which the miners rapidly translated into Poodle Dog—and the current edition does its best to maintain the name's tradition for French food and atmosphere. The present owner, Louis Lalanne, is the son of Calixte Lalanne, who ran the most celebrated Poodle Dog of them all, at Bush Street and Grant Avenue in the pre-Fire days. Reasonable.

ROMANOFF'S, Huntington Hotel, California at Taylor streets, ORdway 3-5642. Open nightly except Sunday from 6 P.M. to midnight. No stockholder's expense has been spared to make this a truly elegant restaurant, all the way from the gold-papered foyer to the darkly seductive bar to the sweepingly wide staircase that leads to the main dining room—a many-splendored dream of banquettes, heel-clicking waiters, and, at various intervals, "Prince" Michael Romanoff (né Gerguson) himself, up from the Hollywoods to observe life in his big-city branch. The food is in keeping with all this magnificence. And all à la carte, of course. The menu is only for the bilingual—volaille poêlée, poussin en cocotte grande mère, délices de sole Duglère, par example—but the prices are easy to decipher: Expensive. There is also an entree enticingly titled "Breast of Young Capon Nob Hill," which somehow sounds like the last sad fate of an unwary debutante, but perhaps I'm being overly sensitive.

SABELLA'S CAPRI ROOM, 2766 Taylor Street, GRaystone 4-8770. Open Monday through Friday from 11 A.M. to 2 A.M., Saturday from 4 P.M. to 2 A.M., Sunday from 1 P.M. to midnight. There is dinner-dancing nightly except Sunday from 9 P.M., at which hour the federal amusement tax and a small minimum charge are added. This ornate upstairs fish emporium features a regular dinner, an à la carte list from A (for abalone) to Z (for zordfish), and even—sound the trumpets— a "New Improved Oysters Rockefeller à la Sabella." This should put the Rockefellers back on the rocks. Prices reasonable, even for an old unimproved Vanderbilt.

SAM'S GRILL, 374 Bush Street, GArfield 1-0594. Open daily Monday through Friday from 11 A.M. to 8:30 P.M. Bar. Another old-timer—Sam's was born in 1867—that goes in heavily for fish. The menu, all à la carte, is as long as the list of Sam's devotees. Almost every kind of fish you can think of, plus things like Hungarian goulash with noodles, chicken à la king with French pancakes, veal porterhouse with bacon. Sam's is not expensive.

SCHROEDER'S, 240 Front Street, GArfield 1-4778. Closed Saturday and Sunday. Open weekdays for lunch—for men only—and dinner, when women, escorted, are welcome, too. Bar. Authentic German atmosphere, complete with tall steins and murals depicting life in the Fatherland in what we assume were the good old days. If you're rootin' for Teuton food, Schroeder's has lots of it—well-prepared and inexpensive. Everything à la carte. Some Schroeder specialties: sauerbraten with potato pancakes, schweizer bratwurst with red cabbage, wiener backhun, wiener and paprika schnitzel, baked spareribs and sauerkraut, garlic sausage and lentils. *Ja wohl!* Inexpensive.

SHADOWS, 1349 Montgomery Street, EXbrook 2-9823. Open nightly for dinner from 5 P.M., Sunday from 4 P.M. Bar. A comfortable Telegraph Hill landmark with a good view of the Bay and the bridges—and, if you can drag your eyes back to the menu, a host of German-style specialties. The dinners always start with soup served family style. Sample entrees: Sauerbraten mit Kartoffel Pfannkuchen, Wiener Schnitzel Garniert, and Kalbs Bries'chen in Brauner Weintunke. Also turkey, chicken, prime ribs, and steak. Plus German beer in your favorite shade. Reasonable.

SHANGHAI LIL, 1020 Kearny Street, SUtter 1-3400. Open nightly from 5:30 P.M. to 3 A.M. (2 A.M. on Sunday). Bar. Mary Tong, a reasonably accurate facsimile of Milton Caniff's Dragon Lady, swishes around this dark little rendezvous in fine, slit-skirted style, and you will probably see at least one movie or stage star lurking in a corner. The food is mainly Chinese, of course, but if you want ham and eggs or steak, they're available too. A popular hangout for the late-late crowd. And if you're dying to hear "Melancholy Baby," there's a pianist on duty. Inexpensive.

SHERATON-PALACE HOTEL, Market and New Montgomery streets, EXbrook 2-8600. Open daily for breakfast, lunch, and dinner. If you would get the feel of old San Francisco at its elegant best, have at least one luncheon in the vast and impressive GARDEN COURT, with its great pillars, its chandeliers, and its multilingual Continental staff, led by its veteran general of waiters, Adolph Steinhof, and the renowned chef, Lucien Heyraud. No matter whether you order the côte d'agneau sauté Malmaison or the boiled New England dinner—the food is superbly prepared—and if there is anything your little heart desires that isn't on the menu, chef Heyraud will probably be glad to whip it up for you. One of the Court's specialties is the Green Goddess Salad, which, to lapse into hucksterese, has been often copied, never duplicated. There is also, of course, a first-rate wine list, with sommelier to match, and a staggering array of fancy desserts which a pastry chef will display at your table, much in the manner of an upper-bracket milliner showing his latest creations. Expensive, naturally. In the same hotel there is the GRILL ROOM, featuring some of the same delicacies as the Garden Court, at slightly lower prices; the PIED PIPER, a luncheon rendezvous for men, where Maxfield Parrish's original "Pied Piper" hangs above the bar in all its dated glory; an excellent coffee shop; and the PALACE CORNER, an intimate room for luncheon and dinner, with dancing in the evening to a small orchestra. The Palace, taken over fairly recently by the Sheraton chain, owes much of its reputation to its food, and it is to the credit of the Sheraton people that they have made no attempt to lower the standards. May it always be so.

SORRENTO, 314 Columbus Avenue, SUtter 1-5037. Closed Monday. Open daily at 4 P.M., closes Friday and Saturday nights at 3:30 A.M. and at 2 A.M. on the four other nights. Beer and wine only. A typical pizzeria, and if you're a pizza fan, you'll enjoy watching the cook fling the dough up to the ceiling, catch it on his fist, and beat the bejabbers out of it. The end result is uniformly excellent. Also a good baked lasagne and veal Parmigiana. And for dessert the Italian delicacy known as canoli (a crisp, crunchy pastry shell filled with ricotta, candied fruit, and chocolate).

TADICH GRILL ("The Original Cold Day Restaurant"), 545 Clay Street, SUtter 1-9754. Open daily except Sunday from 11:30 A.M. to 8:30 P.M. Bar. This simple, unadorned landmark goes all the way back to the magic year of 1849—and its mystifying subtitle derives from the fact that in the 1880's it was the headquarters for a politician named Alexander Badlam, who was wont to boast "It'll be a cold day when I get left."

The cold day arrived in due course, but Tadich's goes on, specializing in fish. Quality high, prices reasonable.

TAJ OF INDIA, 825 Pacific Avenue, EXbrook 2-0089. Open Sunday through Thursday from 5 P.M. to 10 P.M., Friday and Saturday to 11 P.M. Bar. Indian food prepared in the northern or Punjabi manner. There are curries, of course, plus such unpronounceable specialties as suar wuala waag (pork and puréed greens), kofta aur pulao (herb meatballs and savory rice), and keema aur pulao (minced meat with raisins and almonds). If you have any questions—and you will have —owner Harnam Singh will be glad to answer them in the most urbane manner imaginable. (There are two French-American dishes on the menu for the less exotically minded.) Prices reasonable.

TAO YUEN, 823 Clay Street, YUkon 2-7034. Open 4:30 P.M. to 1 A.M. daily except Thursday. No Bar. An unprepossessing basement restaurant with bright lights, bare marble-topped tables, and a fine reputation among Chinese gourmets. Excellent quality all around, and reasonable prices.

TARANTINO'S, 206 Jefferson Street at Fisherman's Wharf, PRospect 5-5600. Open daily for lunch, cocktails, and dinner. Bar. J. Eugene McAteer, a San Francisco politico of note, owns this thriving second-floor sea-food emporium, and he couldn't have been more politic in his choice of location. Tarantino's huge picture windows open out on a handsome view of the wharf's fishing boats, the Bay, and the Golden Gate Bridge. The food is all à la carte—rex sole or sand dabs meunière, filet of sole en papillote, butter-fried crab legs (excellent), for example—and for those who want the view without the fish there are steaks and chops. In short, Tarantino's has a long menu, and a pleasantly brisk, successful air. Reasonable.

TIKI BOB'S, Post and Taylor streets, ORdway 3-5857. Open daily from 5 P.M. to 2 A.M. Bar. The owner, Bob Bryant, learned his craft at the knee of the master, Trader Vic himself, and has come up with a passable imitation of the master's choices: barbecued steaks and chickens, Polynesian hors d'oeuvres, a long line-up of rum drinks, and so on. Atmosphere: dark and pleasant. Prices: not unpleasant, even in the light.

TOKYO SUKIYAKI, 225 Jefferson Street at Fisherman's Wharf, PRospect 5-9030. Open daily for lunch and dinner. Cocktail lounge. The authentic Japanese décor, imported from across the Pacific, is magnificent, and so are the kimono-clad lovelies who serve you. Warning: Check your stockings for holes before you enter, because you'll be asked to remove your shoes once you settle down on the grass mats to eat. Complete luncheons and dinners in the moderate range, including sukiyaki, tempura, soup, salad, baby abalone, tea or coffee. In the à la carte department there are rib steak teriyaki and chicken teriyaki, among other things. And, of course, those

Mme. Butterflys, swaying prettily, to do the actual cooking at your table.

TOMMY'S JOYNT, 1101 Geary Street, PRospect 5-4216. Open daily except Sunday from 11 A.M. to 2 A.M. Bar. This is a "character" place—the No. 1 character being the brash owner, Tommy Harris—that occupies a garish red-and-white Victorian monstrosity sharing a block with a used-car lot and St. Mary's Cathedral (loud cries of "Ah, San Francisco"). Rich dolls in mink coats and greasy mechanics from the nearby garages stand in line for the main attractions: huge corned beef, roast beef, pastrami, and turkey sandwiches. A lot for your money, as Mr. Harris will be the first to tell you.

TORTOLA, 1237 Polk Street, ORdway 3-2636. Open daily from 10 A.M. to 10 P.M., Sundays and holidays from noon to 10 P.M. Service bar. *Aficionados* of the moment of truth in Spanish eating are full of *oles* and refried beans about this landmark in Polk Gulch—and the owner, Mrs. Scarpulla, has an equally high regard for her handiwork. Her pets: Fuera del Mundo, which means "out of this world" and seems to be a little bit of everything; Mission Dolores, an array of enchiladas, cheese, rice, chili con carne, tacos, etc.; and Pancho Villa, which is slightly less of the same. Not expensive.

TRADER VIC'S, 20 Cosmo Place, PRospect 6-2232. Open nightly from 5:30 P.M. to 1 A.M. Bar. In my opinion one of the world's great restaurants. The Trader—his name is Victor Bergeron—

has an intense interest in and passionate devotion to the art of *haute cuisine,* and out of this dedication has grown a restaurant that ranks with the finest anywhere. Unlike some of his successful contemporaries, he refuses to rest on his considerable laurels. Instead he experiments continually with new and exciting dishes, and likes nothing better than a challenge (make him a bet that he or his big crew of French and Chinese cooks can't prepare your favorite dish, whatever it may be, and you'll likely lose). Vic built his reputation originally on Chinese and Polynesian dishes, but don't let that limit your thinking. His French cookery is in a class with New York's Le Pavillon and France's Les Pyramides, and I defy any restaurant in the world to touch the steaks, chops, spare ribs, and fowl that emerge in crusty splendor from his great Chinese barbecue ovens. Vic's menu is long and varied, and if you get cozy with the waiter captains (or the Trader himself), you'll be put privy to delicacies that aren't even listed. There are marvelous hors d'oeuvres, such as rumaki, crab Rangoon, stuffed shrimp, and lobster mousse. Intriguing soups (one of the best, I think, is Bongo Bongo, a cream of puréed oysters). And a host of unusual entrees, among them barbecued Indonesian lamb roast, veal Cordon Bleu, a veal steak stuffed with prosciutto and cheese; mixed grill Calcutta style, butterfly steak Hong Kong style, and kidneys Martinique flambé with sour cream. Besides all these there are dozens of fish dishes, authentic curries, and a seemingly endless array of Chinese and Polynesian specialties. As you may have surmised, Vic's selection is tremendous, and his after-theater menu alone is longer than most restaurants' regular menus. And as you may also surmise, there is almost no limit to what you can spend—but don't let this scare you away. If you order wisely, you can keep your tab down to $5 a person or even less. One last word: Vic is justifiably famed for his rum drinks, served in everything from huge bowls to glasses with stems of naked ladies and festooned with gardenias and real pearls. A final last word: If you have only a night or two in San Francisco, try Trader Vic's. The maître d'hôtel is Bill Coleman, who will TRY to get you a table.

VANESSI'S, 498 Broadway, GArfield 1-0890. Open daily from 11 A.M. to about 3 A.M. Bar. A North Beach landmark, presided over by Joe Vanessi, a man who goes 'way back, knows almost everybody in show business, and treats them all with a charmingly brash disrespect (he once saw Marlene Dietrich seated at the counter and announced loudly: "It cost me fifty dolla' to see you in Las Vegas. Now you come here and see *me* for a forty-cent hamburger!") Next to Joe, the best show at Vanessi's is provided by the cooks working over roaring fires behind the counter, and you might want to sit there to watch their hammy antics, which include chasing one another with cleavers. Regular dinners until 10 P.M. After that, everything à la carte. Good hamburgers on French bread, Joe's Special and minestrone. Moderate.

VENETO, 389 Bay Street, GArfield 1-9711. Open nightly for dinner from 4 P.M., Sunday from 2 P.M., lunch Monday through

Friday from 11:30 A.M. Bar. A fairly picturesque old landmark, a particular luncheon favorite of Tired Businessman and Harried Civic Official types who like to slip away from the downtown area and splash around a bit in Veneto's oversized martinis. Prices moderate to fairly expensive.

YAMATO SUKIYAKI HOUSE, 717 California Street, DOuglas 2-2938. Open daily for lunch and dinner. Cocktails. A beautifully appointed room where you eat on the floor—after first removing your shoes, of course—and there's another section with tables and chairs for those with strong Occidental habits and weak backs. (It is not uncommon to find the Occidentals squatting on the floor and the Orientals dining happily at the tables.) Japanese food fanciers favor the regular dinner, which includes suimono soup, vegetable salad, fried shrimp, sukiyaki, rice, green tea. Also à la carte items. An excellent restaurant, reasonably priced.

City of Hotels

WILLIE BRITT   "I'd rather be a busted lamppost on Battery Street, San Francisco, than the Waldorf-Astoria."

On a per capita basis San Francisco has the country's largest collection of first-class hotel accommodations, a fact that, along with the weather and scenery, contributes largely to its eminence as a convention center. And yet, strangely enough, no major hotel has been built in the city since 1928, when the Sir Francis Drake was opened.

The hotel has played an integral part in the city's life from the Gold Rush days, when the streets were thick with mud and a miner was willing to pay $10 for a place to flop in a "hotel" that was little more than a large tent. One of the first hostelries of note was Buckley's "What Cheer House," on Sacramento Street, which featured "Delousing Rooms for Miners." Another memorable inn that contributed greatly to the city's reputation was the Baldwin Hotel, at the corner of Market and Powell streets, built by E. J. "Lucky" Baldwin in

1876 and destroyed by fire in 1898 (the site is now occupied by the twelve-story Flood Building, named for Baldwin's Bonanza King contemporary, James C. Flood).

But it was William C. Ralston's Palace Hotel that first made the world conscious of San Francisco's coming of age. In the years before its completion, in 1875, Ralston spoke so wildly of its wonders-to-be that a columnist of the *News-Letter* was moved to predict: "It will cover eleven hundred and fifty-four square miles, six yards, two inches . . . A contract is already given out for the construction of a flume from the Yosemite to conduct the Bridal Veil thither, and which it is designed to have pour over the east front . . . The beds are made with Swiss watch springs and stuffed with camel's hair, each single hair costing 11 cents . . . There are 34 elevators in all—four for passengers, 10 for baggage and 20 for mixed drinks. Each elevator contains a piano and a bowling alley. In the dining room, all the entrees will be sprinkled with gold dust."

This hotel confirmed all predictions, even some of the sardonic ones. But Ralston was not around for the grand opening. Shortly before the hotel's completion he went swimming in the Bay off North Beach, as was his daily habit, and drowned. Some claimed he committed suicide because of financial reverses (he owed the Bank of California $4,000,000 on the Palace alone). However, to this day his descendants insist he was merely overexcited, and that the plunge into the Bay's icy waters caused a heart attack.

Senator William Sharon, Ralston's half-hearted associate

("Where is this going to end?" he kept asking his extravagant partner), became proprietor of the Palace, and was soon basking in the reflected glory of such guests as Grant, Sheridan and Sherman, Oscar Wilde, James J. Jeffries, and the city's leading madams, who brought their prettiest girls to the Palace for lunch, where they might catch the eyes of prospective customers.

Even royalty was goggle-eyed. "Nothing makes me ashamed of Brazil so much as the Palace Hotel," said Brazil's Emperor Dom Pedro II in 1876. Royalty died at the Palace, too (King David Kalakaua of Hawaii on January 20, 1891). And in 1906, during the Fire, the old Palace itself died, shaken and then burned to death. Through the quaking halls and out into the street ran the badly frightened Enrico Caruso, carrying a portrait of Theodore Roosevelt, and wearing a towel around his famed throat, vowing loudly never to set foot in San Francisco again. He didn't, although—add little-known facts—he was all set for a triumphal return to the city in 1922 when death intervened.

(Note: Motels, a comparatively recent innovation in land-starved San Francisco, have been springing up all over the city recently. I will not attempt to supply a complete list, for most of them charge approximately the same prices and are as similar as the water-color reproductions on their walls. You will find most of the newer ones on Lombard Street, west of Van Ness Avenue, on Van Ness itself, and on and near the approaches to the Bay Bridge and Bayshore Freeway. There are also elegant ones in San Mateo County—notably the

San Francisco and The Golden Gate Bridge

spanking-new Villa Garden Hotel on El Camino Real in San Mateo, and Rickey's on El Camino Real in Palo Alto—and a rapidly growing collection of "garden hotels," or super-motels, in Marin County and the East Bay.)

Following is a selected list of San Francisco's leading hotels of today, plus a few of the "garden hotels" that feature such added attractions as swimming pools, eating facilities, and bars. As with the restaurants, prices are a problem. The best I can do, hopelessly, is interpret "expensive" as indicating anything from $10 upward to the stratosphere; "moderate" to "reasonable" as $5 to $10 nightly, and "inexpensive" as $5 per night downward. These categories are, I'm afraid, necessarily loose. Allow for a little spillage on both sides.

HOTELS

ALEXANDER HAMILTON, 631 O'Farrell Street, GRaystone 4-5500. Moderate prices. Restaurant and bar. Garage in building. A skyscraper hotel with good views. A few blocks from the shopping and theater districts.

BELLEVUE, 505 Geary Street, GRaystone 4-3600. Prices in the medium bracket. Restaurant and bar. Garage adjoining. Quiet, close to theaters, within walking distance of shopping district.

BERESFORD, 635 Sutter Street, ORdway 3-9900. Dining room open for lunch and dinner only. Garage nearby. One of the better inexpensive hotels.

BEVERLY PLAZA, Grant Avenue at Bush Street, SUtter 1-3566. Tariff: moderate. Dining room, coffee shop, bar. Garages nearby. At the gateway to Chinatown, but not far from main shopping area.

CANTERBURY, 750 Sutter Street, GRaystone 4-6464. Moderate to expensive. Don Burger, a veteran and able hotelman who graduated from Conrad Hilton's staff with highest honors, has transformed this medium-size hostelry into a charming place that will remind you of the chic, sleek smaller hotels of London and Paris. Among its attractions is a lush garden patio ideal for lunching *al fresco* when the weather is not too strongly *al Frisco,* and I can only hope the pun justifies the use of the horrendous word. There is also a well-appointed dining room indoors (see Restaurants) and a bar. Continental tea in the afternoon, and occasional tea- and dinner-dancing.

CARAVAN LODGE, Eddy and Larkin streets, PRospect 6-1380. Prices: moderate to expensive. Bar open nightly until 2 A.M., restaurant open from 7 A.M. to 9 P.M. daily. A lushly appointed de luxe "motel"—you should excuse the expression—with good-sized swimming pool, room service, valet, and with TV in every room.

113

CECIL, 545 Post Street, ORdway 3-3733. Inexpensive to moderate. No dining room. Bar. Garage nearby. A block from Union Square area.

CHANCELLOR, 433 Powell Street, DOuglas 2-2004. Moderate prices. Restaurant and bar. Garage in neighborhood. The Powell cables rattle past the front door, and Union Square is only half a block away.

CLIFT, Geary and Taylor streets, PRospect 5-4700. Dining room (see Restaurants—CLIFT HOTEL REDWOOD ROOM), coffee shop, bar. Garage in adjoining building. An expensive, first-rate hotel, well appointed and well run. The Curran and Geary theaters are in the same block, and the main shopping district is nearby.

COMMODORE, Sutter at Jones Street, TUxedo 5-2464. Restaurant and bar. Garage nearby. A good medium-price hotel, a few blocks from the main downtown area.

DON, 345 Taylor Street, ORdway 3-2332. Coffee shop and bar. Garages nearby. A great favorite with show people appearing in the nearby legitimate theaters. Prices moderate.

DRAKE-WILTSHIRE, 340 Stockton Street, GArfield 1-8011. Rooms moderately priced. Restaurant (the CHARCOAL ROOM —see Restaurants) and bar. Garage in neighborhood. One of the best of the smaller hotels, half a block from Union Square and a few steps away from the finest Post Street stores.

EL CORTEZ, 550 Geary Street, PRospect 5-5000. Not expensive. Room service, bar. Garage nearby. A block from the theaters, two blocks from Union Square.

FAIRMONT, California and Mason streets, DOuglas 2-8800. Expensive, naturally. Seven restaurants (see Restaurants—FAIRMONT HOTEL) and almost as many bars. Garage in building. This handsome granite pile atop Nob Hill was rebuilt in 1907, under the direction of architect Stanford White, after the original structure, started by Tessie Fair Oelrichs as a tribute to her father, James G. "Bonanza Jim" Fair, was all but destroyed in the 1906 earthquake and fire. Today, under the energetic Ben Swig, a comparative newcomer from Boston, the Fairmont is as gay and lively an old girl as you could imagine, without the sacrifice of any of its original grandeur.

FIELDING, 386 Geary Street, GArfield 1-0980. Inexpensive. Dining room, bar. Garage nearby. A busy hotel, only a stone's throw from almost everything.

HOLIDAY LODGE, Van Ness Avenue between Washington and Jackson streets, PRospect 6-4469. Generally expensive. One of the most elaborate of the so-called "garden hotels," with garage, an excellent restaurant and bar, and even a small swimming pool—an innovation that can only be described as daring in San Francisco.

HUNTINGTON, California and Taylor streets, GRaystone 4-5400. Moderate to expensive. Home of "Prince" Mike Romanoff's elegant and expensive new restaurant and bar. Garage in building. On Nob Hill, across the street from Huntington Park, where once stood the mansion of Collis P. Huntington, one of the "Big Four" of the Central Pacific's pioneer days (the other three: Charles Crocker, Mark Hopkins, Leland Stanford).

MANX, 225 Powell Street, GArfield 1-7070. Not too expensive. Bar. Garage nearby. A few steps from Union Square. This hotel's curious name has no connection with the Isle of Man or tailless cats. It was originally the Mann, and the subsequent owner merely found the most inexpensive way possible of changing its name.

MARK HOPKINS, California and Mason streets, EXbrook 2-3434. In a word: expensive. Garage in building. Home of the LOCHINVAR ROOM (see Restaurants), the KILTIE BAR, the PEACOCK LOUNGE—and, most important, the internationally renowned TOP O' THE MARK, the eighteenth-floor bar with a justly celebrated view that is especially effective at sunset. The vista from this glass-enclosed room is so intoxicating that alcohol seems almost superfluous—and yet people *do* drink there; the Top o' the Mark reputedly does more business than any other bar in town, and is known among the *cognoscenti* as "the gold mine in the sky." According to a recent survey, the Top o' the Mark is almost as potent a tourist attraction as Alcatraz, another bar-type institution.

MAURICE, 761 Post Street, ORdway 3-6040. Moderate prices. Restaurant and coffee shop. No bar. Garage adjoining. An attractive medium-size hotel, a few blocks from the main business district.

OLYMPIC, 230 Eddy Street, GRaystone 4-8100. Not expensive. Restaurant, bar. Garage in building.

PLANTATION INN, 3100 Webster Street, WAlnut 1-5520. Another of the city's many de luxe motels, complete with heated swimming pool, a patio with palm trees (imported at great expense), TV in every room, and complimentary "continental" breakfasts, if you give a continental for breakfast. Near the Lombard Street approach to the Golden Gate Bridge. Prices moderate to fairly expensive.

PLAZA, Post and Stockton streets, SUtter 1-7200. Prices in the medium to expensive range. Restaurant (EL PRADO—see Restaurants), coffee shop, bar. Union Square Garage across the street. A good hotel in one of the city's most favorable locations for shopping and general strolling about.

RICHELIEU, Van Ness Avenue and Geary Street, ORdway

3-4711. Inexpensive. Restaurant, bar. Garage in building. Located on "Auto Row," not far from Civic Center, the Opera House, San Francisco Museum of Art.

ROOSEVELT, 240 Jones Street, PRospect 5-6700. Moderate prices. Garage next door. Not the most favorable location in town, but an extremely pleasant, well-run, family-type hotel for all that.

ST. FRANCIS, Powell between Geary and Post streets, YUkon 6-2131. Restaurant (MURAL ROOM—see Restaurants—HOTEL ST. FRANCIS), coffee shop, three bars including one for men only. Connected to Union Square Garage via underpass. The city's largest hotel, gray, weather-beaten and imposing in the Italian Renaissance manner. Originally built in 1904, it was destroyed in the 1906 earthquake and fire and rebuilt in 1909. Some of the town's most distinguished citizens maintain apartments here, and its lobby has been a meeting place for decades (meeting "under the clock" in the St. Francis is as robust a tradition as meeting under the clock at the Biltmore in New York; the clock in question is an Austrian mammoth near the entrance to the Mural Room, controlling fifty smaller clocks throughout the hotel). The St. Francis has one of the country's largest collections of flags, and whenever a visiting foreign dignitary is stopping at the hotel, the flag of his country is flown over the entrance. A favorite Powell Street pastime is trying to identify the St. Francis's flags, usually with no success whatever. Expensive? Quite.

SHERATON-PALACE, New Montgomery and Market streets, EXbrook 2-8600. Expensive generally. Five restaurants (see Restaurants), three bars. Garage across the street. When the original Palace was opened in 1875, it was described as "the world's grandest hotel"—and it undoubtedly was, rising seven stories, containing eight hundred rooms, and playing host for a quarter of a century to kings, emperors, presidents, and mere millionaires. Its ornate wonders (W. & J. Sloane opened its San Francisco store merely to furnish it) perished in the 1906 holocaust, and the present eight-story structure opened in 1909, not quite so earth-shaking as its predecessor, which was at least four times too big for its time and place, but satisfactorily magnificent, all the same. Here, in 1923, President Warren G. Harding died in the presidential suite, and here, no matter what the year, grandeur still reigns in its glass-roofed GARDEN COURT. In 1955 the hotel was purchased by the Sheraton chain from a descendant of Senator William Sharon, who had opened the original hotel almost eighty years earlier. It is now the Sheraton-Palace, but to San Franciscans it is, and always will be, the "Palace."

SIR FRANCIS DRAKE, Powell and Sutter streets, EXbrook 2-7755. Moderate to expensive. Three restaurants (see Restaurants—HOTEL SIR FRANCIS DRAKE), three bars including a sky room, the STARLITE ROOF, with a first-rate view of the downtown area and the Bay. Garage in building. The twenty-two-story Drake (hardly anybody bothers with the "Sir Francis" any more) was built in 1928, but is, nevertheless, the town's newest major hotel. Named after a pirate, it is a block from the St. Francis, named after a saint.

STEWART, 351 Geary Street, SUtter 1-7800. Moderate prices. Two bars, restaurant adjoining, Union Square Garage nearby. A block from the theaters and main shopping centers.

WHITCOMB, 1231 Market Street, UNderhill 1-9600. Prices inexpensive to moderate. Dining room, coffee shop, bar. Garage in building. The Whitcomb, which served just after the Fire and Earthquake as the City Hall (these words are still visible above the marquee) is across the street from Civic Center and near the Opera House and principal movie houses.

Life After Dark

NEWSPAPER CORRESPONDENT, CIRCA 1855   "Hail to the San Franciscan, whose cool climate both fosters a desire for liquor and enables him to carry it!"

San Francisco has changed much through its hundred-odd turbulent years—it has grown respectable, though not quite staid—and its night life has kept steady pace with its march toward urbanity.

In the 1850's all was madness, as befitted the city that "no coward ever set out for, and no weakling ever reached." Gambling joints abounded, there were literally hundreds of saloons serving booze around the clock, and the miners caroused in houses of prostitution of all shades (the fanciest was "The Countess," where full dress was "obligatory," more or less, and six ounces of gold dust, or $96, was the tariff for an evening's pleasure).

But as the years rolled on and the city began to take itself seriously, social lines were more strictly drawn. The gentlemen began withdrawing into the more elegant saloons, where the riffraff was not permitted, and there were soon fancy balls at the Palace and the St. Francis, and in the garish castles of Nob Hill.

However, all these early strivings for respectability went for nought—for down along Pacific Street and its immediate neighborhood the infamous Barbary Coast was flourishing. Named by seamen after the wild and woolly Barbary Coast of North Africa, this sector, with its dance-hall girls and dives where sailors were "shanghaied," contributed largely to San Francisco's reputation as "the wickedest city in the world."

The "Coast" flourished for almost fifty years. But the 1906 Fire burned the heart out of it, and Prohibition gave it a decent burial. The open, go-to-hell wickedness of San Francisco was gone forever.

Speaking of Prohibition, there are those who remember that era rather wistfully. If you can believe their rose-colored recollections, the city had the finest collection of speak-easies west of New York. One of the best—the Philosophers Inn— flourished right across the alley from the Hall of Justice. There were others that featured the best food in town and which, after Repeal, turned into restaurants that are still among the city's finest.

In recent years respectability has become the order of the night in the onetime "wickedest city," but there was (and is) more activity per capita than you'll find anywhere else in the country. In the 1920's, Art Hickman, the composer of "Rose Room," made history with the first really "jazzy" dance orchestra at Hotel St. Francis, and a whole generation grew up to Anson Weeks's music at the Mark Hopkins. And up to a very few years ago there were "name" dance orchestras in the five leading hotels, and lavish floor shows in as many first-rate night clubs.

Of late there has been a new trend in night life that is peculiarly San Franciscan—the sort of *avant-garde*, Left Bank club with canvas chairs and candlelight and almost continuous entertainment. In the face of entertainment taxes and the necessary cover charges the formal night clubs and the big dance orchestras have all but disappeared—and the "character joints" seem to be taking their place.

But the native color that was born with San Francisco dies hard, and night life here can never be completely prosaic, despite the best or worst efforts of the reformers, the zealots and the ever-more-restrictive laws. The city has thirteen hundred-odd bars, and some of them are very odd indeed. And although the curfew rings down its iron curtain at 2 A.M., there is still a tiny buzz of activity through the pre-dawn hours.

Don't look at *me*. I'm a law-abiding citizen. But if 2 A.M. is much too early for you to call it a night, have a word with your bellhop or cabdriver. Who knows? You may learn something.

Following is a list of the better and/or better-known night spots of San Francisco. The 15-per-cent tipping rule applies in most of them, and you can dress pretty much as you please —except that sport clothes for the men are generally frowned upon. And in the larger places it's a good idea to phone first for reservations.

FLOOR SHOWS, WITH DINNER-DANCING

BIMBO'S 365 CLUB, 1025 Columbus Avenue, GRaystone 4-0365. Open nightly. Cocktails from 5 P.M. in the TROPHY ROOM, dinner from 6 P.M., dancing from 7 P.M., floor shows at 8, 10:30, and 1 A.M. There is a cover charge, but you get a good run for your money. This is the city's largest and plushiest night club, run in fine hang-the-expense style by Agostino "Bimbo" Giuntoli, a onetime Palace Hotel janitor who has made very good indeed (he wears a diamond "365" in his buttonhole and has "Bimbo" in gold letters on the back of his Cadillac). The food is good, the drinks are honest, the show girls are tall and the chorus girls are appropriately frisky at Bimbo's—besides which there is the somewhat-famed "Girl in the Fishbowl," a mirror illusion in which a live, nude girl appears, greatly reduced, to be swimming in a revolving bowl of water. Her appearances attract quite a crowd of swimming enthusiasts.

CHINESE SKY ROOM, corner of Pine Street and Grant Avenue, YUkon 2-0486. Open nightly except Thursday from 6:30 P.M. to 2 A.M., shows at 9, 11, and 12:45 A.M. Besides the entertainment there is dancing to a small group in this roof-top rendezvous perched several stories above Grant Avenue. Not too expensive.

FACK'S II, 960 Bush Street, PRospect 6-6360. Open nightly except Tuesday from 8 P.M. to 2 A.M. Generally a door charge and minimum. Three shows on week nights, four on weekends. An attractive room featuring such headliners as Mel Torme, the Four Freshmen, and June Christy—the emphasis, you see, being on modern jazz. No food, but plenty of liquid nourishment and attractive waitresses to supply it. Moderate.

FORBIDDEN CITY, 363 Sutter Street, DOuglas 2-6550. Open nightly except Sunday from 6:30 P.M. to 2 A.M. Shows at 8:45, 10:45, and 12:45. Cover charge. The first, biggest, and best-known of the city's all-Chinese night clubs, run with bubbling enthusiasm by Charlie Low, who acts as doorman, greeter, master of ceremonies, and loquacious introducer-of-celebrities in the audience. When Mr. Low opened this caravanserai in the late 1930's, there was an uproar in Chinatown, and the sages fanned themselves agitatedly over the shocking idea of Chinese girls showing their limbs in public. Now, however, it is all taken as matter of course—and the newer crop of sages can sometimes be seen at ringside tables, gazing admiringly at the Oriental pulchritude in the floor shows. Along with the spectacles, the liquor, and the Chinese décor there is an extensive menu of Oriental and American food. Moderate.

GOMANS' GAY 90S, 345 Broadway, SUtter 1-1899. Open
nightly except Sunday from 5 P.M. till 2 A.M. Floor shows at
8 P.M., 10:30 P.M. and 12:30 A.M. Cover charge. Extensive
dinner menu, and good food, moderately priced. There is
much hustle-bustling in this bright, attractive and newish
club, run with a firm family hand by Bee and Ray Goman,
who graduated from vaudeville years ago but have lost none
of their enthusiasm for the medium. Ray, sporting handle-bar
mustaches out to his ears, and Bee, gowned in glittering creations that Lillian Russell would have swooned over, head the
rollicking floor show—which also includes their son, Ray K.
Goman, who cracks jokes that were old when his parents
were young, but makes them sound funny all over again. A
line of chorus girls, a honky-tonk piano in the bar, community singing for the "Sweet Adeline" set, paper mustaches—
and dancing to a sturdy Dixieland band. Thanks to the
Gomans, who are old-fashioned to the point of thinking the
public deserves a fair shake, this is one of the city's better
night-club values.

SINALOA, 1416 Powell Street, SUtter 1-9624. Open nightly except Wednesday from 5 P.M. until 2 A.M. Shows at 8:30,
10:30, and 12:45. Cover charge. This more-than-typically
"typical" Mexican cantina is well into its second decade of
noisy dedication to castanets and marimba music—a record
for San Francisco night clubs and a tribute to the wise management of Señora Luz Garcia. The Sinaloa is as smoky,
lively, and crowded with characters as any place you're likely

to encounter South of the Border—and the floor shows run heavily to sleek-haired tenors who bellow "Granada" and flashing-eyed señoritas stomping around in floor-splintering flamencos. When the mood is just right, things can get pretty exciting at the Sinaloa, and even in low gear it generates a highly spiced slice of atmosphere. Mexican food, too. Reasonable.

VENETIAN ROOM, Fairmont Hotel, Mason and California streets, DOuglas 2-8800. Open nightly except Monday from 6 P.M. to 1 A.M., shows at 9:30 and midnight. Cover charge. The elegantly decorated (by Dorothy Draper) Venetian Room features "name" entertainment of the caliber of Lena Horne, Sammy Davis, Jr., Nat "King" Cole, the dancing Champions, and the Mills Brothers—but not all in the same show, more's the pity. The food is varied and expensive, and there is dancing to Ernie Heckscher's orchestra, a fairly formidable institution in itself.

ENTERTAINMENT, NO DANCING

ANN'S 440 CLUB, 440 Broadway, YUkon 2-6534. Open nightly except Monday from 4 P.M. to 2 A.M. No cover charge, no door charge. Almost continuous entertainment, starting at 9:30. This small North Beach *boîte* is a "showcase" for young talent, some of it good enough to be snatched by the larger spots and even, occasionally, a Broadway producer. Now and then owner Ann Dee, a onetime New York cabaret singer, leaves the cash register to lend her voice to the proceedings, which are usually fast, furious, and even funny.

BOCCE BALL, 622 Broadway, SUtter 1-9507. Open nightly from 8:30 P.M. to 1:30 A.M. No cover charge, no door charge. If you delight in the more popular operatic arias, you'll hear them sung here in fine-spirited fettle by various tenors, sopranos, and baritones—some of whom are of professional operatic caliber and all of whom plunge into their chores with mucho gusto. The Bocce Ball is genuinely North Beach and, when the crowd is simpatico, as gay and rollicking as the street scene from *Boheme*. The name of the place? It derives from the bocce-ball court out back, where you may watch the *paesani* playing this ancient Italian bowling game.

FINOCCHIO'S, 506 Broadway, DOuglas 2-9913. Open nightly except Sunday from 8 P.M. to 2 A.M. Shows at 9 P.M., 10:45 P.M. and 12:45 A.M. Door charge. This is the far-famed or ill-famed place—depending on your point of view—where "female impersonators" go through their paces, alarmingly disguised in garish wigs, overflowing gowns, and comic-opera false bosoms, all designed to make your visiting maiden aunt from Anamosa, Ia., gasp in delighted disbelief ("You mean they are actually *men*?"). Some of the talent is quite good, and the productions show more imagination than you might expect. Finocchio, incidentally, means "fairy" in Italian. Reasonable.

HUNGRY I, 599 Jackson Street, EXbrook 7-0929. Open nightly from 5 P.M. to 2 A.M., shows practically continuously from 9 P.M. on, dining room open 5:30 to 11 P.M. Door charge to entertainment section. This vast subterranean cavern, which began its night life as a resolutely *avant-garde* hangout for hungry intellectuals (hence the name), has by now achieved a sort of nationwide fame as the forerunner of a new trend in cafés. That is, the emphasis is away from the swank and heavily on the off-beat—both in appurtenances (mobiles dangle in the smoky air, the audience sits in canvas chairs, the waitresses wear their hair and earrings long) and in entertainment (the "I's" brightest product is the young comedian, Mort Sahl, a self-confessed egghead who seldom lays an egg). Along with the large entertainment room there is a good-sized restaurant, a mile-long bar, and still another room —called, with precious simplicity, "The Other Room"—where struggling artists display their wares. By now the Hungry I has become such an established port of call that San Franciscans of all strata patronize it—but there are still a few thong-sandaled, shaggy-haired types in the corners, left over from the nights when the hungry intellectuals alone kept the owner from starving. The owner, incidentally, is a frenetic type named Enrico Banducci, who has never been seen in public (or private, for that matter) without his black beret. Whatever this headgear conceals, it most certainly is not a hole in the head. Reasonable.

LA CASADORO, 720 Broadway, EXbrook 2-9570. Open nightly from 8:30 P.M. to 1 A.M. No door or cover charge. Where else but in San Francisco, may I ask, will you find a saloon where the bartender will suddenly charge out from behind his plank and burst into a highly creditable rendition of "Vesti la giubba" from *Pagliacci*? This happens almost nightly, when barkeep Jack Ghilarducci feels in the mood—and I should add that the mood is practically always upon him, and that his repertoire is almost as long as his fortissimo is high, wide, and shattering. At least three other singers of operatic ditties are always on duty at La Casadoro—and if you feel like joining in a chorus from *Barber of Seville*, go ahead. It's that kind of place.

PURPLE ONION, 140 Columbus Avenue, SUtter 1-0835. Open nightly except Sunday from 8 P.M. to 2 A.M. Door charge. Another pioneer off-beat, *avant-garde*, and/or existentialist cellar, with a more or less continuous show featuring folk singers, monologists (notably the adroit Jorie Remes, who uses the Onion as her home base), and comics of the cerebral variety. Inexpensive.

DANCING, NO SHOW

CIRQUE ROOM, Fairmont Hotel, Mason and California streets, DOuglas 2-8800. Open nightly for dancing from 9 P.M. to 2 A.M. No cover or minimum charge. The adjoining Circus

Lounge, one of the oldest post-Prohibition rendezvous in town, is open most of the day and more than half the night. There is also dancing in the hotel's Chinese restaurant, the TONGA ROOM, to Jack Ross's excellent music.

LOCHINVAR ROOM, Hotel Mark Hopkins, Mason and California streets, EXbrook 2-3434. Dancing nightly except Sunday from 9 P.M. to 1 A.M. Bob Wellman's orchestra supplies the rhythms here, and the constant accompanying babble is set up by a seemingly built-in array of debs and post-debs, all getting their first taste of night life at "The Mark," as their parents did before them.

PALACE CORNER, Sheraton-Palace Hotel, Market and New Montgomery streets, Exbrook 2-8600. Dancing nightly except Sunday from 9 to 1 A.M. Cover charge Saturday only. An attractive, dimly lit room with a cheek-to-cheek atmosphere. Anson Weeks, the most venerable name in the world of San Francisco dance music, is generally in charge of festivities.

STARLITE ROOF, Hotel Sir Francis Drake, Powell and Sutter streets, EXbrook 2-7755. Dancing nightly except Sunday from 9 P.M. to 1:15 A.M. No cover or minimum charge. If you trip over your partner's feet while gliding around the floor in this roof-top spot, it's probably because you're staring out the window at the spacious view of nighttime San Francisco. But let's try not to be clumsy about it, shall we?

STRICTLY FOR JAZZ

BLACKHAWK, 200 Hyde Street, GRaystone 4-9567. Open nightly except Monday from 8 P.M. to 2 A.M. Minimum and door charge depending on the size of the performers' names (and salary). If you're a devotee of the "cool" or "progressive" school of popular music, this is the place for you. Dave Brubeck, the bespectacled progressivist, makes the Blackhawk his headquarters, and when he isn't around to pound, there is usually someone of the caliber of Shorty Rogers, André Previn, and others of their through-the-sound-barrier ilk.

HANGOVER, 729 Bush Street, GArfield 1-0743. Open nightly except Sunday from 8:30 P.M. to 2 A.M. No cover or minimum. The music here is strictly from Dixie, as performed by some of the most eminent two-beaters in this venerable trade: Earl "Fatha" Hines, Muggsy Spanier, Ralph Sutton, for examples.

TIN ANGEL, 987 Embarcadero, SUtter 1-2364. Open nightly except Sunday from 8:30 P.M. to 2 A.M. Door charge. The décor is wackily off-beat in this waterfront spa, but the music is two-beat, and the practitioners are almost always first-rate. The most off-beat character in the place will undoubtedly turn out to be the owner, Miss Peggy Tolk-Watkins, who doesn't know much about Dixieland but has quite a knack for creating a carnival atmosphere.

BARS WORTHY OF NOTE

BUENA VISTA, 2765 Hyde Street, GRaystone 4-5044. Open daily from 10 A.M. to 2 A.M. The "Irish Coffee" craze that has swept the country the past few years originated in this fairly unprepossessing Bayside saloon, which seems to be motley-thronged at all hours with socialites, newspapermen, drifters, dolls, and members of the sports-car set. The Buena Vista serves lunch and dinner, too, a fact that the Irish Coffee swillers seem only dimly aware of. Incidentally, it is located on the site of the first Indian settlement in early-day Yerba Buena, if you think that makes any difference. It doesn't, really.

EL MATADOR, 492 Broadway, GArfield 1-3348. Open nightly from 5 P.M. to 2 A.M. Novelist Barnaby Conrad, author of the best-selling *Matador,* is the guiding spirit here, and the walls of this attractive spot are covered with authentic paraphernalia of the bull ring, plus an impressive array of bullfight art (including a large, full-length oil portrait of the late Manolete, painted by Mr. Conrad). "The Mat," as its *aficionados* fondly call it, is the town's favorite nightcap spot. The man at the piano in the far corner is John Cooper, who might play your request if he isn't occupied in a chess game with one of the Mat's regulars.

Powell Street Cable Car Turntable,
San Francisco

TOP O' THE MARK, Hotel Mark Hopkins, Mason and California streets, EXbrook 2-3434. Open daily from 10 A.M. to 1 A.M.
Few views in the world equal the ecstatic expanse of sea, sky,
hills, and cities visible from any corner of this great bar—and
no matter what time you get there or which picture window
you sit by, you will be enthralled. The sunset hour is generally the most spectacular—but the miles of twinkling lights
late at night are pretty compelling too, and you might find

the place a little less crowded. There is no food service or dancing at the Top, but the view makes both of these items unnecessary anyway.

VESUVIO, 255 Columbus Avenue, DOuglas 2-9808. Open daily from 5 P.M. to 2 A.M. In San Francisco, the bohemian and neo-existentialist bars come and go, but Vesuvio, one of the Old Originals, seems to go on forever, thanks to its ingratiating owner, Henri Lenoir, a beret addict from way back. Mr. Lenoir, who has more humor than most of his contemporaries, calls himself "Trader Henri," has a sign in his window proclaiming "Booths for Psychiatrists," and shows what he calls "color television" (hilarious color slides of old-fashioned postcards, mainly romantic). The works of local artists line the walls, as do the artists themselves—although, adds Mr. Lenoir, "our clientele is not confined to bohemians, thank God!" The bartender, by the way, is Luke Gibney, long one of the city's more respected artists. Definition of "respected": He asks for, and gets, a high price for his work.

BALLROOMS

EL PATIO, 1545 Market Street, MArket 1-1469. Closed Monday and Tuesday, open 8 P.M. to midnight Wednesday and Thursday, 8 P.M. to 1 A.M. on weekends. Old-fashioned dancing Thursday and Sunday, modern Wednesday, Friday, and Saturday, mambo from 2 P.M. to 6 P.M. on Sunday. Not expensive.

The Landmarks

GOLDEN GATE PARK

There are dozens of beautiful parks in San Francisco, but when a San Franciscan says, "Let's go out to the park," he can only mean the 1017 delightful acres of Golden Gate Park. And on a sunny Sunday it seems as though the whole city is there. Automobiles inch along the Main Drive (the speed limit is fifteen miles per hour), families picnic in the grassy, tree-shaded dells (there are no "Keep off the Grass" signs), young lovers float dreamily about in the small boats of Stow Lake, children frolic in a rambling playground of their own, and in the Music Concourse the Municipal Band plays on. And on.

There is a feeling of agelessness in the park, and yet this man-made miracle—four miles long and nine city blocks wide —is actually less than ninety years old. The man who wrought the miracle was a dour, dedicated Scotsman named John Mc-

Laren (everybody called him "Uncle John"), who, in 1887, took over the job of transforming a desolate area of wind-swept sand into a public park second to none in the world—and the lush evidence of his spectacular success grows on every inch and in every corner.

"Uncle John," a benevolent despot who brooked no interference from anyone, ran the park with a green-thumbed iron fist until his death, at ninety-seven, in 1943. During his fifty-six-year reign he planted well over a million trees and acres of tough beach grass to hold the shifting sands, created lakes and wild canyons, brooks and waterfalls, and did his job so fast and so well that by 1894 the park was ready for the world to marvel at as the scene of the California Midwinter International Exposition.

No landmark of the city has given so much pleasure to so many people as this evergreen wonderland, cutting its wide swath from the shadow of the skyscrapers to the rim of the Pacific. Proud peacocks strut along its shady glens, and chattering squirrels dart up to grab a peanut out of your hand. Thousands of waterfowl glide around its artificial lakes, and buffalo and elk roam across its man-made hillocks. More than five thousand varieties of plants grow in the park: towering redwoods, Monterey pine and cypress, a hundred kinds of eucalyptus, cypress from Kashmir, abelias from the Himalayas, daisies from South Africa—and thousands upon thousands of rhododendrons comprising the world's greatest collection (over three hundred varieties and four hundred hybrids) of this plant.

The park is dotted, too, with dozens of statues—much to the dismay of the late "Uncle John," who fought each and every one, and, when he lost the fight, succeeded in partially hiding them behind shrubbery, at least. Only one statue in the park stands in full view, undisguised by so much as a leaf. Ironically, it's a statue of "Uncle John" McLaren—erected after he was no longer around to protest.

Finding specific points of interest in the park is not easy on your first visit. However, you can get information and maps at the Park Lodge, near Stanyan and Fell streets. And perhaps this rule of thumb will be helpful:

Entering the park from the Stanyan (city) side, you will find the following, more or less in order, on the south (or left) side of the Main Drive:

Kezar Stadium (home of the professional 49ers football team), Children's Playground, bowling green, tennis courts (twenty-one of them), baseball diamonds, De Young Museum, Academy of Sciences, Steinhart Aquarium, African Hall, Music Concourse, Strybing Arboretum and Botanic Garden, Japanese Tea Garden, Stow Lake (for boating), Strawberry Hill (above Stow Lake, and the highest point in the park), Golden Gate Park Stadium (polo grounds), fly-casting pool, recreation field (for soccer, mainly), the Murphy Windmill (one of the park's two Dutch windmills) and, as you reach the ocean, the forty-seven-ton sloop *Gjoa*, given to the city in 1909 by her commander, Roald Amundsen, the noted arctic explorer who discovered the Northwest Passage and fixed the location of the North Magnetic Pole.

You will find the following on the north (or right) side of the Main Drive:

The Conservatory, modeled after the Royal Conservatory in Kew Gardens, London; Lloyd Lake and the Portals of the Past (all that remained of the Nob Hill mansion of A. N. Towne after the 1906 fire-quake); Spreckels Lake, headquarters for migratory birds and miniature yachting enthusiasts; Buffalo Paddock and Elk Glen, where the deer and the buffalo roam, seemingly at large (the fences are artfully concealed); the Chain of Lakes, the North Windmill, and, just beyond, the ocean.

If you have time for only a short stay in the park, you will be most rewarded in the area surrounding the Music Concourse, south of the Main Drive. Here you will find:

ALEXANDER F. MORRISON PLANETARIUM, open from 10 A.M. to 5 P.M. daily. Projections of the skies at various times during the week, for a nominal admission charge; for exact information, phone BAyview 1-5100. However, admission to the building and its many unusual exhibits is free. Opened in 1952, this planetarium features the first projector (of the heavens) ever made in this country. The six others in U.S. planetariums were made in a German factory that is now in the Russian Zone. No matter what your age or inclinations, you will find this a fascinating exhibit.

NORTH AMERICAN HALL, open daily 10 A.M. to 5 P.M., no admission charge. Large collection of American mammals, displayed in an approximation of their natural habitat. Also large game fish, birds, trees, minerals, stones, reptiles, and so on.

SIMSON AFRICAN HALL, open from 10 A.M. to 5 P.M. daily. No admission charge. This beautiful hall and its spectacular display of African wild life was collected and presented by Leslie Simson, a mining engineer-sportsman who made many African expeditions. You will be most impressed, I think, with the representation of an African water hole, surrounded by impalas, giraffes, zebras, gnus, gazelles, and hartebeests. Other exhibits show lions, baboons, gorillas, leopards, and many others, all displayed most dramatically against extremely effective backgrounds.

DEPARTMENT OF ENTOMOLOGY, second floor of African Hall, contains more than a million mounted insects. In the basement of the same building is the Department of Ichthyology, with half a million specimens of fish.

STEINHART AQUARIUM, open 10 A.M. to 5 P.M. daily, no admission charge. Easily the most popular attraction in the park, the aquarium draws as many as ten thousand visitors a day, all walking around openmouthed in the semi-darkness to stare at the openmouthed fish. This handsome building, presented to the city in 1923 by Ignatz Steinhart, contains about twelve thousand fish—just about everything that swims except Esther Williams. A shed behind the aquarium contains the skeleton of a seventy-five-foot sulphur-bottom whale, plus skulls of several smaller leviathans.

JAPANESE TEA GARDEN, open 10 A.M. to 5 P.M. daily, no admission charge. This idyllic five-acre corner of the park was opened during the 1894 exposition and has charmed generations of visitors with its winding paths, its streams crossed by stone bridges, its pools aglow with goldfish, its "wishing bridge," and its flowering quince, cherry, and plum trees. Tea and cakes are served in the thatched teahouse.

THE MUSIC CONCOURSE features concerts by the Municipal Band, 2 to 4:30 P.M. Sunday and holidays, no admission charge. This outdoor, sunken auditorium seats 20,000 people. And being outdoors, concerts are automatically canceled by inclement weather.

DE YOUNG MEMORIAL MUSEUM (see A World of Culture).

Other points of interest:

STOW LAKE, where you may rent rowboats, canoes, and small electrically powered boats.

CHILDREN'S PLAYGROUND, where the children will have a field day on the merry-go-round and swings, on the Shetland-pony rides, and in the miniature farm, featuring live animals.

STRYBING ARBORETUM AND BOTANIC GARDEN, directly across the South Drive from the Japanese Tea Garden, covering forty acres of land, more than twenty of which are under intense cultivation and contain more than three thousand different kinds of plants, all growing in the open—a sizable tribute in itself to San Francisco's weather; scientists and botanical students from all over the world come to marvel—and you might well do likewise.

SAN FRANCISCO ZOOLOGICAL GARDENS

This great zoo, on Sloat Boulevard at Forty-ninth Avenue, is open 10 A.M. to 4:30 P.M. daily, no admission charge. Launched in 1924 by contributions of money and animals from financier Herbert Fleishhacker, the zoo now covers some seventy acres and houses a notable collection of elephants, lions, bears, giraffes, tigers, leopards, lynxes, panthers, birds, and so on. Some of these roam about in large open areas, separated from the spectators by only a moat—and the illusion of freedom is very real indeed. The seals, who put on an amusing show, are fed at 1:30 and 4:30 P.M. daily. The lions are fed at 2 P.M. daily except Monday, and the elephants are fed at 3:30 P.M. daily. The zoo was originally named Fleishhacker Zoo, and on a crowded Sunday it was not uncommon to hear a small child tugging at his mother and asking, "Mommy, where are the fleishhackers?"

Adjoining the zoo is Fleishhacker Pool, the world's largest

outdoor salt-water swimming pool, open daily 9 A.M. to 5 P.M. (Admission: 50¢ for adults, 10¢ for children under eighteen.) In some unkind quarters, this is known as Mr. Fleishhacker's "white elephant," since its vast area (it's 1000 feet long, 150 feet wide) is seldom filled—and besides, the Pacific Ocean is only a few steps away. Nonetheless it's one hell of a big swimming pool.

OCEAN BEACH

"The Beach"—roughly the seaside area between Sloat Boulevard and the Cliff House—is a vast expanse of sand heavily populated on warm days by large women in small bathing suits, small women in large bathing suits, proud-muscled young men in practically nothing but biceps, and children and dogs, most of them having fights with one another. Warning: Swimming is dangerous off Ocean Beach. There's a vicious undertow just beyond the breakers, and the annual death toll is depressingly high.

Across the 200-foot-wide Great Highway from the beach is Playland-at-the-Beach, which, along with the neighboring Cliff House, Sutro Museum and Ice Rink, various rides, and gift shops, was built by one man: George K. Whitney. Playland-at-the-Beach is a not so small edition of Coney Island, with everything from spun sugar on a stick to jolting rides that'll make you sorry you ate the stuff. The Cliff House serves food and drinks (see Restaurants) and has a magnificent

Seal Rocks and the Cliff House ... San Francisco

view of Seal Rocks and the ocean. Sutro Museum is jammed
with mementos, fascinating and otherwise, offering convinc-
ing proof that the late Mr. Whitney never threw anything
away.

Seal Rocks are about four hundred feet offshore from the
Cliff House, and contain no seals whatever. Only sea lions
by the hundreds. If there aren't any visible at the moment,
they're probably off somewhere mating. Sea lions love sea
lions, which is convenient because nobody else could.

Atop the bluff directly above the Cliff House is Sutro
Heights, once the magnificent estate of Mayor Adolph Sutro,
who built his mansion there in 1870 (it was torn down in
1939). Mayor Sutro, who seems to have been a most unusual
man, opened his parklike grounds to the public, and a sign
at the entrance invited the people "to walk, ride and drive
therein." Today nothing remains but the trees, the lawns, the
broken statuary, and fading memories of a gentler era.

THE ISLANDS

THE FARALLONES: These islands—seven in the southern group and a smaller group seven miles to the north—lie twenty-six miles off Ocean Beach, and are the inspiration for San Francisco's sturdiest cliché: "On a clear day, you can see the Farallones." Presumably the few people who live on these forbidding rocks remark that "on a clear day, you can see San Francisco." Southeast Farallon, the most important island in the chain (it's a mile long and half a mile wide), is occupied by about two dozen men of the Coast Guard, manning the lighthouse, fog signal, and radio. These islands are closed to the public.

ALCATRAZ: This island in the Bay—the famed "Rock" of many a B movie—is also closed to the public; or, at least, a large segment of the public. Its federal penitentiary houses several hundred "incorrigible" prisoners, plus guards and their families. Alcatraz was discovered in 1775 by Lieutenant Juan Manuel de Ayala, who named it Isla de los Alcatraces (Isle of the Pelicans) because he found so many of these birds nesting there. A much tougher bird dwells there now—but, contrary to public opinion, at least three of them *have* flown the coop. In 1920, Roy Gardner, "The Gentleman Bandit," escaped alone from Alcatraz and got away with it—and in 1938, two prisoners swam away and presumably reached the mainland safely too. At least their bodies were never found.

ANGEL ISLAND: This is the largest island in the Bay—about a
mile square and almost directly behind Alcatraz, near the
Marin shore. It's a lovely place to picnic—if you have the
yacht to get you there.

YERBA BUENA ISLAND: The bore that connects the suspension and cantilever sections of the San Francisco-Oakland
Bay Bridge passes through this rocky, heavily wooded island.
Originally known as "Goat Island," Yerba Buena is now occupied by the admiral of the 12th Naval District and other
high Navy brass. No admittance except by pass from 12th
Naval Headquarters, Federal Building, San Francisco.

TREASURE ISLAND: Twenty million tons of sand and mud were
dredged from the Bay to form this man-made island, the
scene of the 1939–40 Golden Gate International Exposition.
Connected by causeway to Yerba Buena, it is now a Navy
base. Likewise not open to the general public.

THE BRIDGES

SAN FRANCISCO-OAKLAND BRIDGE: The world's longest
bridge (twelve miles, including approaches) was completed
in November 1936 at a cost of $77,000,000, and is a veritable
hotbed of staggering statistics: its massive concrete central

anchorage is equal in height to a forty-story building, its towers are 700 feet high, clearance above water is 216 feet, and the tunnel through Yerba Buena Island, connecting the suspension and cantilever spans, is the largest-diameter tunnel in the world. The bridge has six lanes for automobile traffic in its upper deck and three lanes for bus and truck traffic, plus two tracks for electric trains on the lower deck. When the bridge is jammed at rush hours with commuter traffic, you can understand why San Francisco wags sigh, "The bridge is long enough, but not wide enough." Toll charge: 25¢ per auto, and the toll collectors always say, "Thank you."

GOLDEN GATE BRIDGE: This, the longest single-span suspension bridge in the world, was opened in 1937—and was something of a bargain: it cost only $35,000,000, a sum that will buy practically *nothing* these days. Serene and graceful, it stands as a tribute to engineer Joseph B. Strauss, the five-foot giant who refused to accept the long-accepted opinion that bridging the Gate was "impossible" (because of the swift tides). Its statistics are also dizzying: the bridge is 8981 feet long, and measures 4200 feet between its two great towers, which rise 746 feet above high tide (the height of a 65-story building); its center span is 220 feet above water. That's a long jump for the 173 known suicides (at this writing) who have leaped to their death from "The Bridge of Size"—and it's interesting to note that Bridge authorities figure privately that at least as many more suicides have jumped undetected. Toll charge: 25¢ per auto.

Old Fort Point and
the Golden Gate Bridge

RICHMOND-SAN RAFAEL BRIDGE: Opened on August 31,
1956, this peculiarly humpbacked span, the world's second
longest over-water bridge (4.04 miles), brings the Contra
Costa and Marin shores within five minutes of each other;
the ferries it replaced took 25 minutes. Toll charge: 75¢ per
auto.

CHURCHES OF INTEREST

CALVARY PRESBYTERIAN CHURCH, Jackson and Fillmore
streets. Built in 1901, this church houses the city's largest
Presbyterian congregation.

CHURCH OF STS. PETER AND PAUL, 666 Filbert Street. Its
tall graceful twin spires make this Roman Catholic church
one of the most attractive houses of worship in the city. The
mosaics on either side of the doorway show Dante at work on
his Paradiso and Columbus landing in the New World.

FIRST UNITARIAN CHURCH, corner of Geary and Franklin
streets. This ivy-covered, quietly dignified edifice was dedicated in 1889. In its tiny churchyard is the white marble
sarcophagus of Thomas Starr King (1824–64), the militant
pastor whose rousing speeches helped swing California to the
side of the Union in the Civil War.

GRACE CATHEDRAL, California, Taylor, Sacramento, and Jones streets. This massive group of buildings, looking as ancient and timeless as any Gothic church in Europe, houses the first cathedral seat of the Protestant Episcopal Church in America, and occupies the site of the old Crocker mansion. Its establishment dates back to 1865, when the Rt. Rev. William Ingraham Kip, first Episcopal bishop of California, placed his seat in the original Grace Church, destroyed in the 1906 fire. The present church, still unfinished (the spire has yet to be completed), was begun in 1914. The north tower contains a carillon of forty-four bells which can be heard for many blocks in all directions, much to the annoyance of late Sunday sleepers (and no sympathy for them!).

HONGWANJI BUDDHIST MISSION, 1881 Pine Street. First Buddhist church in America. In the roof-top shrine are three tiny bone fragments, reputed to be portions of the body of Buddha, and presented to the church in 1935 by the King of Siam.

OLD ST. MARY'S CHURCH, Grant Avenue and California Street. This Gothic landmark was opened in 1854, and was the heart of Catholicism in California until the opening of St. Mary's Cathedral. Now run by the Paulist fathers, it has daily services at noon as well as the usual early morning Masses.

ST. FRANCIS OF ASSISI, 610 Vallejo Street. Named for the city's patron saint, this church was founded in 1849 as

Old Saint Mary's Church
San Francisco

the first Roman Catholic parish in San Francisco. On the front steps stands sculptor Beniamino Bufano's eighteen-foot statue of the saint, which had reposed in a Paris warehouse for twenty-five years before the parishioners arranged to have it shipped to San Francisco and erected in 1955.

ST. IGNATIUS CHURCH, corner of Fulton Street and Parker Avenue. Straight out of the Renaissance is this beautiful church, with its twin towers, its campanile, and its gleaming golden dome. Alongside St. Ignatius are ranged the buildings of the University of San Francisco, conducted by the Jesuits. The university (formerly St. Ignatius College) accepts male students of all denominations; the law and evening classes are coeducational.

ST. MARK'S EVANGELICAL LUTHERAN CHURCH, O'Farrell Street between Gough and Franklin streets. First Lutheran church in California, dedicated in 1849. Until 1931 services were conducted here in German. The present building, dedicated in 1895, is of Romanesque design.

ST. MARY'S CATHEDRAL OF THE ASSUMPTION, corner of Van Ness Avenue and O'Farrell Street. Seat of the Roman Catholic Archbishopric of Northern California. A large red brick edifice of German Gothic design, completed in 1894.

TEMPLE EMANU-EL, Lake Street and Arguello Boulevard. Religious and cultural center of Reformed Judaism in San Francisco. Designed in the form of an "L" enclosing an open court with cloisters and fountains. The auditorium seats 1700.

TEMPLE SHERITH-ISRAEL, Webster and California streets. Pioneer center of Reformed Judaism, built in 1904 for a congregation organized in 1850.

TRINITY EPISCOPAL CHURCH, corner of Gough and Bush streets. The first church of its denomination founded on the Pacific coast (in 1849), Trinity Episcopal is now housed in an impressively Norman structure, built in 1892. The founder of the church, Rev. Flavel Scott Mines, who died in 1852, is buried beneath the chancel.

OTHER POINTS OF INTEREST

PORTSMOUTH SQUARE, Kearny Street between Clay and Washington streets. One of the city's most historic spots. Here on July 9, 1846, Captain John B. Montgomery first raised the American flag. And here, in 1879, sat Robert Louis Stevenson, coughing his slight cough and turning his thin face to the sun. He is remembered by a monument—the first ever erected in his honor—surmounted by a bronze galleon, the *Hispaniola* of *Treasure Island*.

FISHERMAN'S WHARF, foot of Taylor Street. This fragrant and picturesque little section of the waterfront is more than just

San Francisco's Fisherman's Wharf

the locale of a dozen or so sea-food restaurants. It is basically
the heart of a thriving fishing industry, served by over two
thousand men and 300 boats, bringing in hundreds of thousands of pounds of fish in a year: sole, salmon, sand dab, crab,
sardines, rock cod, and flounder, to name the most numerous.
If you're interested in doing a little deep-sea fishing of your
own, boats are usually available for hire—so haggle away.

AQUATIC PARK, Polk and Beach streets. A white, streamlined
structure built by the WPA in the late 1930's, and resembling
a ship at anchor. The building, along with affording a splen-
did view of the Bay and Alcatraz, houses a first-rate Maritime
Museum. This exhibit is maintained by the San Francisco
Maritime Museum Association, which also maintains, at Pier
43 (near Fisherman's Wharf), the *Balclutha,* last of the great
Cape Horn sailing fleets. This square-rigger, built in Scotland

159

in 1886, was restored in 1955 by a yearlong community effort, in which eighteen Bay Area labor unions donated 13,000 hours of work, and almost 100 business firms gave $100,000 in supplies and services. Admission charge: 50¢ for adults, 25¢ for children.

PRESIDIO OF SAN FRANCISCO, main entrance Lombard and Lyon streets. A beautiful parklike area of some one thousand five hundred acres at the northwestern tip of the city. It is usually open twenty-four hours a day, and well worth driving through. The Presidio, now headquarters of the Sixth Army and site of the largest military hospital in the West (Letterman General), has been a fortified area since 1776, when the soldiers of King Charles III of Spain were headquartered there. The present Officers Club is housed in the oldest adobe building in San Francisco, built in 1776. At various times the Presidio has been commanded by Generals William Tecumseh Sherman, John J. Pershing, and Mark Clark.

MISSION DOLORES, Dolores Street between Sixteenth and Seventeenth streets. Open daily 9 A.M.–5 P.M., admission 25¢, children free. Founded by Padre Francisco Palou in October 1776, this amazingly well preserved landmark, one of the chain of California missions, has played a part in San Francisco history from its very beginnings. The first marriages, the first baptisms, the first Christian burials in San Francisco— all were performed here. Buried in the mission's old cemetery are Captain Luis Antonio Arguello, first governor of Alta California under Mexican rule; Charles Cora and James Casey, victims of Vigilante justice (Casey's headstone reads: "May God Forgive My Persecutors"); James "Yankee" Sullivan, a champion among pioneer pugilists, and José Noe, last Mexican alcalde (mayor) of Yerba Buena.

FOR THE SPORTS-MINDED

BASEBALL: National League baseball, featuring the San Francisco Giants, from April through September at Seals Stadium, Sixteenth and Bryant streets, MArket 1-6641. Consult newspapers for schedule.

FOOTBALL: Professional football—San Francisco's team is the 49ers—from August to December at Kezar Stadium in Golden Gate Park. College football at University of California Memorial Stadium in Berkeley, and at Stanford University Stadium in Palo Alto. Again, consult your newspaper for more detailed information.

BOXING: Irregularly scheduled at Civic Auditorium, the Cow Palace, and the Coliseum Bowl. Check sports pages for details.

WRESTLING: On Tuesday nights at Winterland (Post and Steiner streets, WAlnut 1-0112), unless the annual Ice Follies —generally June through July—is in progress.

BASKETBALL: At the Cow Palace (Geneva Avenue and Rio Verde Street, JUniper 4-2480) and at Kezar Pavilion in Golden Gate Park (MOntrose 4-3200).

TENNIS: There are courts in various playgrounds around town, but the most numerous are in Golden Gate Park, and reservations may be made by phone (LOmbard 6-4800). There are private courts at California Tennis Club and the Olympic Club's Lakeside Country Club—if you are lucky enough to know a member.

GOLF: Public courses are Harding Park (par 72) at Lake Merced (MOntrose 4-4690); Lincoln Park (par 69) at Thirty-fourth Avenue and Clement Street (BAyview 1-9911), and Sharp Park (par 72) in Sharp Park, south of San Francisco (FLanders 5-2862).

BOATING: Boats are available in Lake Merced on Harding Road, south of Sloat Boulevard near the zoo. Phone LOmbard 6-8442 for information. There is also boating in Stow Lake in Golden Gate Park (SKyline 2-0347).

HORSE RACING: There are three first-rate tracks around San Francisco, featuring nationally known stables and jockeys. Golden Gate Fields (LAndscape 6-3020) is on the East Shore Highway in Albany and about twenty-five minutes from San Francisco via the Bay Bridge. Tanforan race track (JUno 8-5650) is in San Bruno, about twenty-five minutes from the city via El Camino Real. Bay Meadows (FIreside 5-1661), south of San Mateo, is about forty minutes away via Bayshore Highway. Consult sports pages for schedules.

SKATING: Ice skating at Sutro's at the Beach (1000 Pt. Lobos Avenue, BAyview 1-7711); at San Francisco Ice Arena (1557 Forty-eighth Avenue, SEabright 1-9711), and at Legg's School of Ice Skating (1951 Ocean Avenue, JUniper 6-1300). Roller skating at Skateland at the Beach (Grant Highway at Balboa Avenue, SKyline 4-1747).

CIVIC CENTER, roughly, the area between Leavenworth Street and Van Ness Avenue, McAllister and Grove streets. Grouped around Civic Center Plaza (McAllister, Larkin, Grove, and Polk streets) are (1) the $3,500,000 City Hall, dedicated in 1915, whose magnificent though tarnished dome rises 296 feet, 9 feet higher than the National Capitol's; (2) Civic Auditorium, Grove between Polk and Larkin streets, whose main auditorium seats 10,000; (3) the War Memorial Opera House and adjoining War Veterans' Memorial Building, Van Ness Avenue between McAllister and Grove streets, the latter building containing the San Francisco Museum of Art; (4) State Building, McAllister between Polk and Larkin streets, housing the local offices of the Governor, Attorney General, and other state functionaries; (5) Public Library, Larkin and McAllister streets, containing about 600,000 volumes, with an especially fine collection of works on fine art and music, and manuscripts of such California authors as Gertrude Atherton,

Ambrose Bierce, Bret Harte, Robinson Jeffers, Mark Twain, George Sterling, Joaquin Miller, and Jack London; (6) Federal Building, bounded by Hyde, Leavenworth, Fulton and McAllister streets, where some 1,500 Federal workers are employed. Passports are obtained here; (7) the new underground Convention and Exhibit Hall, known with typical San Francisco irreverence as "Mole Hall."

MONTGOMERY BLOCK, Montgomery and Washington streets. Built in 1853, this four-story structure, built on a foundation of redwood logs, was the only downtown office building to escape destruction in the 1906 fire—and it has successfully avoided destruction by real estate operators ever since, although its existence is threatened with doleful regularity. The "Monkey Block," as it is affectionately known among old-timers, is in the heart of the city's bohemian sector, and in the 1890's its studios housed such notables as Kathleen, Charles, and Frank Norris, George Sterling, and Charles Caldwell Dobie. Here, in 1856, crusading editor James King of William lay dying while angry citizens formed the Vigilance Committee, who hanged his assassin, James P. Casey. And here Dr. Sun Yat-sen plotted the overthrow of the Manchu dynasty.

PALACE OF FINE ARTS, foot of Lyon Street, near Marina Boulevard. This graceful building, one of the most photographed landmarks in the city, is all that remains of the $50,000,000 Panama-Pacific International Exposition of 1915,

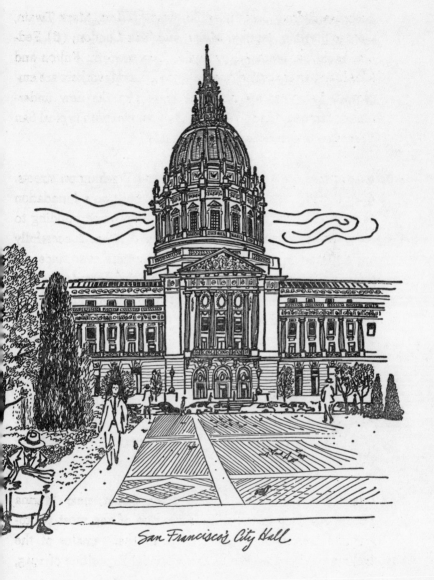

San Francisco's City Hall

during which it housed the fair's art exhibit. Today, its terra-cotta walls are crumbling into the curved lagoon which mirrors its Corinthian columns—but even in its twilight hours, its beauty is a tribute to its designer, architect Bernard Maybeck of Berkeley.

In a Hurry?

RUDYARD KIPLING   "San Francisco has only one drawback
    —'tis hard to leave."

If I had only one day in San Francisco, I would:
    Spend the morning hours strolling through Chinatown.
    Lunch at Fisherman's Wharf.
    Drive across the Golden Gate Bridge to Marin, and, upon
returning, drive along Ocean Beach to Sloat Boulevard and
return to the downtown area via Twin Peaks, with its match-
less panoramic view.
    Have cocktails at Top o' the Mark.
    Dine at Trader Vic's.
    Wind up the evening in the more colorful North Beach
spots—i.e., the Hungry I, the Purple Onion—and have a nightcap at El Matador.

If I had a second day in San Francisco, I would:
    Spend the morning hours visiting Gump's and the Union
Square-Maiden Lane area.

Lunch in the Garden Court of the Sheraton-Palace.

Spend the afternoon in Golden Gate Park, visiting Steinhart Aquarium, De Young Museum, the Morrison Planetarium.

Have cocktails at the Cliff House.

Dine at the Blue Fox, Alexis' Tangier, Jack's, Ernie's, Romanoff's, or Amelio's.

Catch a show, if the attractions sound interesting, in the Fairmont's Venetian Room or the 365 Club. Or if jazz is your forte, find out who's playing at the Black Hawk, Hangover, Fack's, or the Tin Angel.

Have a late snack at the Papagayo Room.

If I had a third day in San Francisco, I would:

Spend the morning hours visiting North Beach, Telegraph Hill, and Coit Tower.

San Francisco's skyline from the new freeway

Lunch at Kan's in Chinatown, or the Yamato or Tokyo Sukiyaki houses.

Take a cruise around the Bay via Harbor Tours.

Have cocktails at the Buena Vista, if you can elbow your way in through the characters.

Dine at Grison's Steak House.

Check to see whether there's an opera or symphony concert at the Opera House, or a good attraction at the Curran, Geary, or Alcazar theaters.

Have a nightcap and a spot of dancing in the Mark Hopkins' Lochinvar Room or the Fairmont's Cirque Room.

If you succeed in doing all this in three days, you will leave San Francisco tired and possibly broke—but secure in the knowledge that you have hit most of the high spots. And I am confident that, like MacArthur, you shall return.

Off the Beaten Path

FRANK NORRIS   ". . . a city where almost anything can
happen."

A city is more than monuments, parks, notable restaurants,
and world-famous hotels. It is also mansions and tenements,
quiet streets and back alleys, tycoons and derelicts—and,
above all, the slightly hidden facets known only to the natives. A few examples:

The old, expansive days of legendary glory may be past, but
San Francisco still does all things—good and bad, in a big
way. Per capita, it has more hotel rooms, more telephones,
higher incomes, and a higher cost of living than any other
city in the land. Also more mental cases, more suicides, and,
especially, more alcoholics. Cirrhosis of the liver is a leading
cause of death in San Francisco, whereas it isn't even among
the first ten killers nationally.

A concomitant of this shame is San Francisco's "Skid

Road," a shabby district of flophouses and pawnshops, seamy bars and grimy lunch counters—and unfortunate people to match. The moocher and the wino are the butt of endless jokes in San Francisco, but the reality is tragic and the problem is critical.

If you are curious for a glimpse of "Skid Road," walk or drive along Howard Street, between Third and Fifth streets. This is not to say there aren't completely respectable people and businesses along these blocks—but you will see enough in the way of human misery (drunks passed out on the sidewalk, tatterdemalion vagrants sleeping in doorways) to give you a lasting impression. And the uncomfortable realization that there is more to San Francisco than spacious views from soaring hills.

For the tourist who sniffs, "Shucks, San Francisco isn't as hilly as I thought it would be," I suggest a drive down Filbert Street from Hyde to Leavenworth. Approach it cautiously, however, because many a spring and an impressive number of bones have been broken on this 37.1-per-cent grade. But fast or slow, you will get a satisfying squeal or scream from the back-seat passengers, for there is a definite sensation of flying into space when you reach the brink of this precipice and plunge over. A homely local joke has it that this street was named Filbert for good reason: only a nut would drive down its awesome hill.

Less frightening but uniquely spectacular is the Lombard Street "curlycue," far-famed as "the crookedest street in the

Skyline from Yacht Harbor, San Francisco

world"—and it may be, at that. This brick-paved street cork-screws down the hill between Hyde and Leavenworth in a series of almost 90-degree turns—and you have to be a good driver to negotiate it successfully. It's a one-way street, so start down from Hyde. And good luck.

The foreign color that abounds in San Francisco is concentrated no more heavily than on Broadway between Columbus Avenue and Powell Street. This is worth a few minutes of your walking time, for along these two blocks you'll find French, Basque, and Mexican restaurants, Filipino barber-shops, a Chinese theater, Italian bars, a French pharmacy—in all, a veritable United Nations in microcosm. In the midst of all this there was, up to a short time ago, an establishment that quite understandably called itself "The Neutral Cleaners." But neutrality pays off no better here than it does anywhere else. "The Neutral Cleaners" went out of business.

If you're up and around at 4 or 5 A.M., and have run out of things to do and see, you might wander down to the produce district—bounded by Pacific, Sacramento, Front, and Drumm streets. This is Mother San Francisco's cupboard, and in the early hours of the morning trucks carrying fruits, vegetables, poultry, and so on begin arriving from the country. The accompanying sights and sounds are colorful indeed, and if you're the gregarious type, you'll meet some interesting characters, too.

For all its glittering past, Nob Hill is not where most of the rich people live. It has, of course, its fashionable hotels and its fairly elegant apartment houses, but the mansions of yesteryear are long gone, and the reputation of Nob Hill today is more legend than fact. The favored district of the favored few is a section that includes Pacific Heights and Presidio Heights, and the boundaries are difficult to discover. However, if you drive west from Fillmore Street along Broadway, Pacific, Jackson, and Washington to about Presidio Avenue, you will get part of the picture. Other attractive residential areas are Sea Cliff, St. Francis Wood, and Forest Hill (west of Twin Peaks), Russian Hill, and Lombard Street as it curves up toward Coit Tower.

Glamorous turn-of-the-century San Francisco was typified by huge wooden homes of a spectacular ugliness, bulging with bay windows and festooned with the kind of scrollwork known as "carpenter's Gothic." Some notable examples of this sorry era still abound in the Western Addition—roughly, the area between Van Ness Avenue and Fillmore, O'Farrell and Broadway. You'll see a few fine old mansions in good repair, a lot of not-so-fine old mansions dying out their days as "guesthouses" (the San Francisco euphemism for boardinghouses), and a lamentable number of decaying dwellings that are nothing more or less than slums. These, however, are gradually being torn down, to be replaced by stern housing projects that are as neat as they are unimaginative. Incidentally, one of the most endearing and best-preserved examples of Victorian architecture in the area is the wooden home of the Fire Department's Engine 15, at 2150 California Street. Architects come from miles around to marvel at its crenelations, its quatrefoils, and its wooden busts of former fire chiefs.

Further odds and ends: *If* it's a warm sunny day, and *if* you brought your bathing suit, and *if* you have no-place to sunbathe, about the only handy places I can suggest are Aquatic Park, at the foot of Polk Street, and the Marina Green, on Marina Boulevard at, roughly, the foot of Scott Street. If you are interested in Bonsai, the unique Japanese art of dwarfing trees, there's an outstanding Bonsai nursery at 2566 California Street, where you are welcome to browse. If you are deeply devoted to Oriental art treasures, Leonid Kosloff has a collection of museum-caliber pieces in his upstairs studio at 555 Sutter Street. If printing is your passion, you might want to drop in at the Grabhorn Press at 1335 Sutter Street, where, in the opinion of some experts, "the world's finest printing" is produced. And if you've always had a burning desire to see how Chinese fortune cookies are made, drop in at Lotus Cakes, 436 Pacific Avenue. The proprietor, Ernie Louie, will be glad to show you how those doubtful Confucianisms wind up inside those tasty little cookies.

A World of Culture

ANON.   "I feel sorry for children born in San Francisco. How
sad for them to grow up and discover that all cities are not
like theirs."

San Franciscans, by and large, are almost ferociously proud
of the cultural heritage that has always played a major role
in the life of "the city that never was a town."

At the drop of a raised eyebrow they point with pride to
their first-rate symphony orchestra, their magnificent War
Memorial Opera House (the first municipal opera house in
the country), the glittering opera season whose opening out-
shines the Metropolitan's, the "popular" opera company (the
Cosmopolitan) which makes a tidy profit each season, the
sellout performances by top-flight concert stars and ballet
companies, the free open-air summer concerts in beautiful
Sigmund Stern Memorial Grove, the three major art museums
that are all or partially supported by city and county funds,
the legitimate theaters whose audiences (so the actors say)
are the most sophisticated in the country, the widespread

"little theater" activity, and the many theaters showing foreign or "art" films exclusively—more, per capita, than any other city in the country.

All in all, a good show in a city that has always been known among performers as "a great show town"—and that has always played enthusiastic host to the great artists of every era.

A hundred or so years ago the city's darlings were Lotta Crabtree, Lola Montez, and Adah Isaac Menckens. Edwin Booth starred here, and so did John Drew and Maurice Barrymore. In turn-of-the-century San Francisco, David Belasco laid the foundations for his great career. And a generation of first-nighters threw flowers at little Maude Adams, Adelina Patti, and Sarah Bernhardt, "cooing, cursing and dying" in one hundred and thirty roles.

It was here that vaudeville enjoyed its golden age at the Orpheum on O'Farrell Street, with such headliners as Jack Benny, Al Jolson, Ted Lewis, Eddie Cantor, and Sophie Tucker. It was here that "Doc" Leahy, manager of the old Tivoli Opera House, made a star of Luisa Tetrazzini, the city's most beloved prima donna ("Chicken Tetrazzini" is still on many a restaurant menu). And it was at the Tivoli, in 1913, that Leoncavallo conducted his own *I Pagliacci*.

San Francisco has known and loved them all. Ferde Grofé, later to write his memorable *Grand Canyon Suite*, pounding a piano in a Barbary Coast dive. Paul Whiteman fiddling away (and badly) at the Fairmont Hotel. The great American composer, Ernest Bloch, serving for long years as head of the San Francisco Conservatory of Music; and Darius Milhaud, one of the very best of the modern composers, on the teaching staff at Mills College. Yehudi Menuhin, Pierre Monteux, Isaac Stern, and many more, all weaving their particular bright threads into the rich tapestry of San Francisco life.

And it is a pattern that will never end. For in San Francisco the musician, the singer, the writer, the artist—the creative people in all fields—will always find inspiration and encouragement.

WAR MEMORIAL OPERA HOUSE, Van Ness Avenue and Grove Street, UNderhill 1-9200. Opened on October 15, 1932 (with Claudia Muzio in *Tosca*), designed by Arthur Brown,

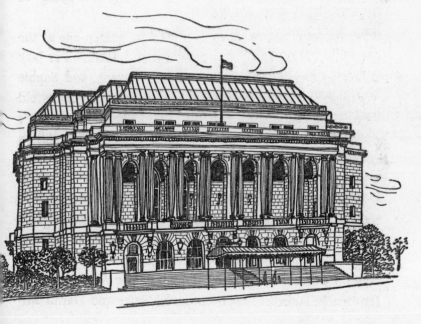

Jr., and G. Albert Lansburgh. Seating capacity: 3,285. The annual opera season, the city's top social event, opens in the middle of September and runs about six weeks, followed by the eighteen-week season of the San Francisco Symphony, under the baton of Enrique Jorda. In the spring the Cosmopolitan Opera Company presents its annual season of popular-priced performances. Between these regular activities are concerts and ballets, both by visiting companies and the San Francisco Ballet, so that the great lights of the Opera House are seldom dark. For details check your newspaper.

SIGMUND STERN MEMORIAL GROVE, Sloat Boulevard at Nineteenth Avenue. During the summer months (roughly, from early June until early September) this grass-carpeted, eucalyptus-shaded natural amphitheater is the scene of free open-air concerts each Sunday afternoon, sponsored by the Midsummer Music Festival Association and featuring members of the San Francisco Symphony, plus various soloists. The concerts start at 2 P.M. and run to about 4:30 P.M., and, with the audience sprawled around on the grass, are a most pleasant way to pass an afternoon—even when the fog starts to roll in, making the musicians work doubly hard to play in tune. Most of this thirty-three-acre glade was purchased by the late patroness of the arts, Mrs. Sigmund Stern, and presented to the city as a memorial to her husband. Along with being a cultural wonderland the grove is a delightful place for picnics, and there are barbecue facilities, too.

LEGITIMATE THEATERS

San Francisco's "theater belt," which once boasted as many as eight first-rate houses running simultaneously, has shrunk considerably of late, owing to the impact of TV and movies and the diminishing number of traveling companies. The "belt" now contains three theaters, and is perhaps more accurately described as a "garter." They are:

CURRAN, 445 Geary Street, ORdway 3-4400. Named for Homer Curran, late impresario. A current Broadway hit is usually on view here, and during the summer months the annual Civic Light Opera Festival is presented, featuring four popular musicals, more light than opera.

GEARY, 415 Geary Street, ORdway 3-6440. Adjoining the Curran, and presenting the same sort of entertainment.

ALCAZAR, 260 O'Farrell Street, DOuglas 2-3636. A grand old name in the city's theatrical history, now operated by impresario Randolph Hale and also featuring current Broadway hits, with the original or road-show companies.

LITTLE THEATERS

They come and they go—the fate of most little theaters—but the ones most likely to be in business, and presenting something experimental or off-beat, are:

ACTOR'S WORKSHOP, 2528 Folsom Street, MIssion 8-9918.

BELLA UNION, 825 Kearny Street, SUtter 1-9909.

PLAYHOUSE REPERTORY, 2796 Hyde Street, PRospect 5-4426.

There are three theaters in Chinatown—(Grandview, 756 Jackson Street, GArfield 1-9233; Great China Theater, 636 Jackson Street, YUkon 2-5498; and Sun Sing, 1021 Grant Avenue, YUkon 2-2448). But if you're interested, you'd better phone first. One never knows.

Leading ticket agencies: Crane Box Office (245 Powell Street, DOuglas 2-4566); Hotel St. Francis (DOuglas 2-2325, YUkon 6-2131); Sherman Clay & Co. (Sutter and Kearny streets, SUtter 1-1331); Ethel Moore (Hotel Sir Francis Drake, EXbrook 2-1801).

MOVIE HOUSES

The leading first-run theaters are grouped along Market Street, from about Fourth Street to Tenth. The "art" houses, featuring road-show "spectaculars" or foreign films more or less exclusively, are:

BRIDGE, 3010 Geary Boulevard, BAyview 1-4022.

CLAY, 2261 Fillmore, FIllmore 6-1123.

CORONET, Geary at First Avenue, SKyline 2-4400, featuring Todd A-O.

FOUR STAR, Clement near Twenty-third Avenue, BAyview 1-2200.

LARKIN, 816 Larkin Street, PRospect 5-3811.

PRESIDIO, 2340 Chestnut, WAlnut 1-2929.

RIO, 2240 Union Street, FIllmore 6-3680.

RITA, 1596 Church Street, ATwater 8-2705.

STAGE DOOR, 420 Mason Street, YUkon 6-4767.

VOGUE, Sacramento Street at Presidio Avenue, BAyview 1-8181. If you haven't seen Cinerama, it's on view at 1192 Market Street, MArket 1-5000.

MUSEUMS

SAN FRANCISCO MUSEUM OF ART, Veterans' Building, Van Ness Avenue at McAllister Street, HEmlock 1-2040. Directed by Dr. Grace L. McCann Morley, this museum, on the fourth floor of the Veterans' Building, pays primary homage to modern art. Its permanent collection includes outstanding examples of the work of Matisse, Picasso, Klee, Léger, Vlaminck, Pollock, Hofer, Epstein, Moore, Braque, Cézanne, Van Gogh, and many others. No admission charge. Open Monday 12 noon to 5 P.M., Tuesday through Saturday 12 noon to 10 P.M., Sundays and holidays 1 P.M. to 5 P.M.

CALIFORNIA PALACE OF THE LEGION OF HONOR, Lincoln Park, BAyview 1-5610. This handsome structure, patterned after the Palais de la Légion d'Honneur in Paris, was presented to the city in 1924 by Mr. and Mrs. Adolph B. Spreckels as a memorial to California's soldier dead in World War I (the inscription beside the main entrance reads: *"Hommage de la France aux héros Californiens mort pour la défense du droit et la liberté"*). One of the five original bronze casts of Rodin's "The Thinker" occupies the main court, and another Rodin masterpiece, "The Shades," a memorial to merchant-philanthropist Raphael Weill, may be seen in the outer driveway. The museum's nineteen main-floor galleries include the works of Fra Bartolommeo, Rubens, Murillo, Velázquez, El Greco, Fragonard, Constable and Reynolds. Director: Thomas Carr Howe. No admission charge. Open daily 10 A.M. to 5 P.M., legal holidays 1 P.M. to 5 P.M.

M. H. DE YOUNG MEMORIAL MUSEUM, Golden Gate Park, BAyview 1-2067. Named in honor of the founding publisher of the San Francisco *Chronicle,* this vast museum houses everything from Egyptian, Greek, and Roman sculptures to items of early-day wearing apparel; from weapons of war to ship models; from arts of the Orient to a noteworthy collection of great classics, including the works of Rembrandt, Rubens, Van Dyck, El Greco, Fra Angelico, Titian, Pieter de Hooch, and Goya. The large central-court walls are covered with four huge Gothic-Flemish tapestries donated by the widow of the late Mr. de Young's onetime arch-rival, William Randolph Hearst. The De Young Museum, oldest and largest municipal art museum in the West, draws almost a million visitors annually, making it the most popular in the world in relation to its population area. Director: Dr. Walter Heil. No admission charge. Open 10 A.M. to 5 P.M. daily.

JOSEPHINE D. RANDALL JUNIOR MUSEUM, Sixteenth Street and Roosevelt Way, UNderhill 3-1399. Open daily from 10 A.M. to 5 P.M. Not strictly a museum, and rather difficult to find (the 43 bus will get you there if you haven't a car), but paradise itself for young people—ages 6 to 21—who like to do things with their hands, learn crafts, play with animals, and so on. Under expert guidance, children can use the looms, polish stones, make ceramics, see movies, run a printing press, take hikes in the nearby hills, and generally have a maximum of instructive fun in a pleasant atmosphere devoid of "Do Not Touch" signs.

Around the Bay

RICHARD HENRY DANA   "San Francisco, the sole emporium of a new world, the Pacific."

San Francisco is the hub of a teeming area that pours thousands of commuters and vehicles into the city every day. If you like figures with your facts, about 120,000 people work in San Francisco daily but live elsewhere. Some 275,000 vehicles enter or leave the city every day. In all there are about 600,000 daily movements to and from San Francisco through the Peninsula, East Bay, and North Bay gateways.

According to the best available figures, some 1,284,000 people live in the counties more or less contiguous to San Francisco. Alameda (the East Bay) claims about 847,000, San Mateo 330,000, and Marin 107,000. Almost half of San Francisco's commuter population lives on the Peninsula, 36 per cent in Oakland and about 15 per cent in Marin.

So much for statistics. I'm sure you're more interested in how you get to these places—and what you'll see, once you're there.

Marin has one immediate advantage over its sister counties. A very few minutes after you enter it via the Golden Gate Bridge, you plunge into what is still, despite the ubiquitous tract builders, "the country." In the spring wild flowers carpet the rolling hills, and there are numerous inviting trails winding through thick stands of redwood, eucalyptus, oak, madrone, and manzanita. From dozens of vantage points thrilling vistas open up—the Pacific gleaming to the west, the Bay spreading out to the east, and San Francisco shining in the distance.

If your time in Marin is limited, I heartily recommend a visit to Muir Woods, a 424-acre preserve of virgin redwoods given to the nation in 1908 by Senator William Kent as a monument to John Muir, the naturalist. You will also be richly rewarded by a drive up the winding road that encircles Mount Tamalpais (altitude: 2604 feet). On a clear day you can see a third of Northern California, and on any kind of day the view is memorable.

You will also enjoy a look at Belvedere, an enchanted isle of spectacular homes just off the Marin shore on the Bay side, and nearby Tiburon. And, of course, do not overlook Sausalito, the hilly village that is closest to San Francisco. For all its artsy-craftsiness Sausalito is a place of infinite charm, and if you don't remark that it puts you in mind of a Mediterranean fishing village, you don't qualify for the Cliché Derby.

Marin's boosters (I've never found a knocker) call the

county "Marvelous Marin." This may sound hyperbolic, but it isn't.

The sprawling world of the East Bay spreads before you as you cross the Bay Bridge. Directly ahead lies the queen city of Oakland (population: over 400,000), with its business section clustered around the seventeen-story City Hall. It is a city of fine homes in the Piedmont and hillside areas, a beautiful lake (Merritt) in the heart of the city, a big Negro section (in West Oakland), three harbors, and the best-known women's college in the West—Mills.

Oakland is also the butt of many San Francisco jokes, although not so many as formerly. It has been called "San Francisco's Brooklyn" (or "Brookland"), and, in the days when it contributed the lion's share of commuters, "San Francisco's bedroom." In the era of vaudeville, performers were heard to observe that "the three worst weeks in show business are Christmas, Easter, and Oakland." And a sign backstage at the hallowed Palace Theater in New York once warned: "If you think you're good, play Oakland."

However, fast-growing Oakland, with its fine airport, its busy waterfront, and its many industries, no longer frets about these gibes. It has its own cultural background too. Here Jack London developed his great talents, proud Joaquin Miller wrote his poetry, and Edwin Markham awoke one morning to find himself famous as the creator of *The Man with the Hoe*. And there are scenic beauties: the panoramic view of the Bay Area from the hills of Oakland—especially at dusk, when the lights are coming on—is one you'll not soon forget.

While you're in Oakland, incidentally, you may want to visit the First and Last Chance Saloon, at 50 Webster Street. Jack London did much of his writing in this rickety old shack, and many of his mementos have been preserved. There is even the gambling table on which he allegedly composed, although this may be in the same class with the desks supposedly used by Mark Twain. And the beds that held George Washington.

To the north of Oakland, and contiguous, is Berkeley (population: about 117,000), famed for its hills and its homes, its college-trained police department—and, of course, the University of California, with some 17,000 students. The city was named for Bishop Berkeley, the Irish philosopher who intoned, "Westward the course of empire takes its way."

North of Berkeley lies Richmond (population: about 92,000), largest city of Contra Costa County, principal West Coast port for the transshipment of oil, and eastern anchor of the new Richmond-San Rafael Bridge to Marin County. Here, during World War II, the Henry J. Kaiser shipyards built 745 Liberty ships.

To the south of Oakland is the city of Alameda (population: about 70,000), located on an island one mile wide and six and a half miles long lying alongside Oakland. As one observer has noted, "Alameda looks something like a violin, with its neck pointed toward the Golden Gate." It is connected to Oakland by several bridges and the Posey Tube under the

Oakland Estuary, which, at the time of its completion in 1928, was the largest underwater tube for vehicular traffic in the world. Alameda is also the home of a $75,000,000 Naval Air Station.

The dominant peak rising in the East Bay is Mount Diablo (altitude: 3849 feet).

San Mateo County—or the "Peninsula"—is served by two main highways, the Bayshore Highway and El Camino Real, or "King's Highway," whose route dates back to the eighteenth century, when it tied together the long line of missions and pueblos of Spanish days. Both highways are designated U.S. 101, but they are quite different.

Bayshore is a high-speed super-highway that skirts the Bay and whizzes past the outskirts of most of the Peninsula cities. In short, if you're in a hurry, take Bayshore—and it's the fact that most of the people on Bayshore *are* in a hurry that makes it dangerous. This is the highway you should take, incidentally, if you want to visit the magnificent $50,000,000 San Francisco International Airport, which ranks among the world's finest.

The easiest approaches to Bayshore, for newcomers, are: Down Stockton Street, across Market and into Fourth Street, which leads directly to the Bayshore Skyway; or down Polk Street, across Market, and into Tenth Street, which also brings you to the Skyway ("skyway" is the city's high-falutin' designation for "freeway").

However, for a more leisurely look at the Peninsula, I recommend El Camino Real, which meanders at a fairly reasonable rate through the whole string of "commuter" communities between San Francisco and Palo Alto. The simplest approach to this highway is straight out Mission Street, the busy artery that runs parallel to downtown Market Street and is one block south of it.

Along El Camino Real you will drive through, in almost endless succession, Daly City and the new development of Westlake, followed by the Colma-Lawndale area of cemeteries. Then come Tanforan race track, San Bruno, Millbrae, Burlingame, and Hillsborough. There are many fine homes and estates in this area, and a right turn at Floribunda Avenue will afford you a quick look at some of them—although you may have to stand on tiptoe to see over the high walls.

Back on El Camino Real you will pass through bustling San Mateo, Bay Meadows race track, Belmont, San Carlos, Redwood City, and Atherton. Atherton is another section of beautiful homes, and a right turn on tree-lined Atherton Avenue will carry you past their imposing gates and beautiful gardens. Another quiet, beautifully wooded settlement in this area is Woodside, and you will find a sign pointing in its direction on El Camino Real in Redwood City.

After passing through Menlo Park you will come to the end of the Peninsula proper in Palo Alto, a pleasant city of fine homes, block after block of magnolia trees (on University Avenue), a gleaming new shopping center (on the highway as you approach the city), and, of course, Stanford University, with its 7500 students, its 90,000-seat stadium, and its easily visible landmark: the Hoover Library for War,

Peace and Revolution, surmounted by a fourteen-story, 280-foot tower and housing ex-President Herbert Hoover's collection of 150,000 manuscripts dealing with World War I and its results.

Two lesser highways serve the Peninsula, and each is notable for its scenic beauties. Skyline Boulevard (State Highway 5) heads south from the Great Highway on the Pacific Ocean front and winds through mile after mile of spectacularly wooded, hilly countryside. Alongside this highway in San Mateo County you will pass the sparkling Crystal Springs Lake, chief reservoir for San Francisco's water supply.

Another exciting route is State Highway 1, which also starts south from the Great Highway and hugs the rugged Pacific shore line on its long journey toward Southern California. If you are heading for the Carmel-Pebble Beach-Monterey area, I recommend Highway 1 as the most interesting approach, by long odds. It's not fast, but you won't feel you've wasted your time.

EATING AROUND THE BAY

Marin County

ALTA MIRA HOTEL, 126 Harrison Avenue, Sausalito, EDgewater 2-1350. Dining room open daily for breakfast from 8 A.M. to 12 noon, luncheon from noon to 3 P.M., dinner from

201

5 P.M. to 11 P.M. The most attractive features of this place are its Sky Room cocktail lounge, with an excellent view of the Bay, and its open veranda, a pleasant spot for luncheon on a sunny day. Moderate prices.

BLUE ROCK INN, 505 Magnolia Avenue, Larkspur, WAbash 4-4171. Open for dinner from 5:30 P.M. to 11 P.M. daily except Wednesday and on Sunday from 4 P.M. Sunday brunch from 10 A.M. to 1:30 P.M. Cocktail lounge open daily from 10 A.M. to 2 A.M. This inn was opened in 1883, and the décor is in keeping with its early heydays and nights. Not too expensive.

CAPRICE, 16 Main Street, Tiburon, GEneva 5-9972. Open nightly for dinner from 5 P.M. to midnight, and from 11 A.M. to 5 P.M. Sunday and Monday for what owner Kirby Atterbury calls "drunch," which sounds suspiciously like a drunken lunch. Beer and wine only, but a long list of the latter, domestic and imported. An attractive candlelit little spot on the main street of this arty Marin village. Mr. Atterbury's dinners are simple but tasteful, and beautifully served. Prices reasonable, unless you start ordering that wine by the gallon.

DEER PARK VILLA, Bolinas Road, Fairfax, GLenwood 3-9916. Open daily from 6 P.M. to 10 P.M., Sundays 4 P.M. Bar. Another Marinstitution, this one featuring Italian food. Regular dinners in the medium range.

GALLI'S, 5929 Redwood Highway, Ignacio, TUcker 3-9911. Open from 5 to 9:30 P.M. daily except Monday, 3 to 9:30 P.M. on Sunday. Bar. People come from miles around for the huge dinners in this Marin landmark. Complete dinners— and I do mean complete. The bar is noteworthy for a huge and presumably valuable collection of ancient bottles, practically none of which has ever been dusted. Reasonable to fairly expensive.

JUANITA'S GALLEY, Gate 5 Marinship, Sausalito (you'll probably have to ask directions), EDgewater 2-9997. A robustly salty hangout, as remarkable for its unorthodox hours as it is for the pugnacious, more or less, personality of its owner, Juanita Musson. Her joint, which caters to the fishing trade, is open Saturday, Sunday, and Monday from 2 A.M. to 6 P.M., and on other days from 2 A.M. to 9 P.M. You pour your own coffee and defend yourself against Juanita's gibes as best you can. Great ham and eggs, and a grand old army of colorful types at all hours.

MARIN JOE'S, Highway 101 at the Corte Madera turnoff, WAbash 4-2081. Open daily from 5 P.M. to 1 A.M. Bar. All à la carte. Moderate.

ONDINE, 558 Bridgeway, Sausalito, EDgewater 2-0791. Open nightly for dinner from 5:30 P.M., Sunday from 2 P.M. The bar and lounge open about an hour earlier. A handsome new establishment on the edge of the Bay, proving that all it takes to transform an old bait shop into a beautiful restaurant is imagination, money, and the old gambling spirit. In this case, the gamble has paid off nicely, for Ondine, with its sweeping across-the-water view of San Francisco and the nearby Marin isles, opened with a full house and hasn't been otherwise since. The food is interesting—generally French—and fairly expensive. But, as I said, a lovely spot.

SABELLA'S, on Highway 101 six miles north of the Golden Gate Bridge, DUnlap 8-6944. Open daily 11 A.M. to midnight. Bar. Dinners à la carte, prices reasonable. Sabella's is the inventor of Craviolis—which, as you might suspect, are ravioli stuffed with crab.

SAM'S, Tiburon, GEneva 5-4527. Open daily except Monday from 9 A.M. to 11 P.M. Bar. An old standby in one of the prettiest corners of Marin. For decades yachtsmen have been docking their boats here and loading up on food and drink before beginning the long trek back across the Bay to San Francisco. The food is substantial—steaks, chops, fish, etc., and the prices are ditto.

VALHALLA, 201 Bridgeway, Sausalito, EDgewater 2-1792. Open from 4 P.M. to 2 A.M. daily except Monday, Sunday brunch starting at 11 A.M. Bar. Sally Stanford, San Francisco's most renowned madam of the present generation until the cops done her wrong, now operates this bustling waterfront restaurant—and its Victorian décor is as authentic as Miss Stanford's racy reputation. Entrees include the usual sea food, steaks and chops, chicken cacciatore, and tenderloin tips flambeau.

The East Bay

A large segment of Oakland's eating places is now grouped in Jack London Square, a fairly recent development at the foot of Broadway on the shores of the Oakland Estuary. Among the restaurants are:

BOW AND BELL, GLencourt 2-3400. Open daily from 11 A.M. until about 11 P.M. (midnight on Friday, 1 A.M. Saturday, Sunday brunch from 9 A.M.). Bar. Owned by Jackie Jensen, the Boston Red Sox outfielder, and Boots Erb, onetime California football star. Huge menu. Á la carte, you can run the gamut from abalone to zabaglione. Reasonable.

OAKLAND SEA FOOD GROTTO, TWinoaks 3-2244. Open daily from 11 A.M. to 2 A.M. Bar. Fish served in all its multifarious forms. Specialty: stuffed turbot. Regular dinners from inexpensive (the ever-lovin' sole) to quite a bit more (the omnipresent steak).

SEA WOLF, HIghgate 4-3456. Open daily from 11:30 A.M. to 11 P.M. A fairly elegant spot, with regular dinners. Reasonable.

Some other Oakland restaurants:

CAPRIOTTI'S, 372 Grand Avenue, TEmplebar 2-1702, open 4 to 11 P.M. daily except Monday. Bar. Specialty: capon Capriotti on the de luxe dinner. Complete dinners, with endless hors d'oeuvres. Moderately priced.

CUISINE PATISSERIE, 4350 Broadway, no telephone, open 5 to 9 P.M. daily except Monday and holidays, Sunday 4:30 to 8:30 P.M. Wine only. An excellent, not too expensive little French restaurant that has only one drawback: 'tis exceedingly difficult to squeeze into.

MITCH'S, 529 Seventeenth Street, GLencourt 1-1724, open 11:30 A.M. to 11:30 P.M. daily except Sunday. Bar. A hangout for Oakland trenchermen who just can't get enough beef. Reasonable to fairly expensive.

OSCAR'S, 3277 Lakeshore Avenue, TWinoaks 3-7670. Open 5 P.M. to midnight daily, 3 to 11 P.M. Sunday. Bar open 10 A.M. to 2 A.M. daily. Dinners with choice of four entrees: prime ribs, New York-cut steak, club steak, barbecued chicken. Moderate.

TRADER VIC'S, 6500 San Pablo Avenue, OLympic 3-3400. Open daily for luncheon from 11:30 A.M., for dinner from 4:30 P.M. Bar. This is the "first" of Trader Vic's now far-flung empire of excellent restaurants, and, despite the fact that the Master no longer has much time to stomp around the premises, the quality is as high as ever. There are several attractive rooms in this Polynesian-style layout, a bar where the rum flows freely, if expensively, and an array of shrunken heads at the entrance. Contrary to rumor, these are *not* the heads of customers who couldn't pay their checks. Defaulters are strung up in the barbecue pits. Reasonable to expensive.

VILLA DE LA PAIX, 116 Sixth Street, TWinoaks 3-7556. Open daily for lunch from 11:45 A.M. to 3 P.M., à la carte service till 5 P.M., dinners from 5 P.M. to 11 P.M. Bar. An attractive spot that is generally jammed, a happy situation that has prevailed ever since this place opened many years ago. Regular dinners and à la carte specialties. Reasonable to fairly expensive.

Berkeley

CLAREMONT HOTEL, Tunnel Road and Domingo Avenue, THornwall 3-3720. Lush gardens surround this beautiful rambling hotel in the Berkeley hills, and it's worth a look-around for aesthetic reasons if for no other. However, if you're thirsty, there's a handsome glass-enclosed cocktail room, and if you're hungry, there's food from 6:45 A.M. on-ward. Dinner-dancing to well-known orchestras on Friday and Saturday.

LARRY BLAKE'S, 2367 Telegraph Avenue, AShberry 3-0886. Open daily from 7 A.M. to 1:30 A.M. Specialty: steak and salad. The basement rathskeller is heavy on sawdusty floors, beer on tap, and campus characters in the corners. Inexpensive.

SPENGER'S FISH GROTTO, 1919 Fourth Street, THornwall 5-7771. Open 11:30 A.M. to 1 A.M. daily. Short on décor but long on sea food and comparatively painless on the pocketbook. A sixty-year-old landmark.

Contra Costa County

In recent years a considerable "restaurant row" has sprung up in the fast-growing Lafayette-Walnut Creek area, reached through the Broadway Tunnel (most direct approach: via Ashby Avenue in Berkeley). For example:

CAPE COD HOUSE, Lafayette, ATlantic 3-8288. Open daily for lunch and dinner. Bar. The emphasis is on fish, and especially on Florida pompano en papillote. Food fanciers in the area have a high regard for this restaurant. Fairly expensive.

ORINDA WILLOWS, Orinda, CLifford 4-4355. Open daily from 11 A.M. to 2 A.M., dinner till 10 P.M., snacks till 2 A.M. Bar and dancing. Reasonable.

TUNNEL INN, Lafayette, ATlantic 3-6251. Open daily from 5 to 11:30 P.M. Bar. The proprietor, Jay Bedsworth, is one of the more accomplished professional magicians, and if you can get him to your table, he'll make everything disappear except the check. The food is as good as his legerdemain. Reasonable.

HOTEL DANVILLE, Danville, VErnon 7-9097. Danville is about seven miles south of Walnut Creek—about forty minutes in all from San Francisco—but a surprising number of people seem to find this place worth the trip. Hotel Danville isn't a hotel at all, but a spacious old spot encompassing four dining rooms. Reservations are advisable. It's a long way to go to find no tables available. Reasonable to fairly expensive.

The Peninsula

CHEZ YVONNE, 1854 El Camino Real, Mountain View, YOrkshire 7-6368. Open Wednesday through Sunday from 4 P.M. to 2 A.M. Bar. Yvonne is a true *Française,* and her food has that authentic Gallic (not garlic) touch. She does fine things with game hen, frog legs, terrine de foie gras truffe, escargots, and, of course, the inescapable onion soup. Dinners are in the moderately priced department, and the lights are so enticingly low you can barely read the check. However, a waiter will be glad to assist.

INTERNATIONAL ROOM, San Francisco International Airport, Bayshore Highway, PLaza 6-1662. Open for lunch daily except Saturday, for dinner nightly from 5 to 11:30 P.M. Bar. From the great windows in this restaurant on the third floor of the city's $50,000,000 terminal you can see planes landing and taking off every minute on the minute. The menu, if you can tear your eyes away from the activity, contains such delicacies as Hawaiian mahi mahi (dolphin), New York steaks, and shish kebab. International, you see. Dinner prices at the medium level, in good old Yankee dollars.

L'OMELETTE, 4170 El Camino Real, Palo Alto, DAvenport 3-8922. Open Wednesday through Saturday 5 P.M. to 2 A.M., Sunday 4 P.M. to 2 A.M. Bar. A pair of wise-eyed, appropriately charming French brothers, André and Pierre Frelier, run this gaily Gallic institution—André performing the Continental bowing and scraping at the door while Pierre mixes singularly lethal martinis behind the big square bar. "L'Ommie's," as les Freliers hopefully believe everyone calls it, is heavily populated with Stanford undergrads, but the food is definitely off-campus: good steak à la minute, coq au vin, coquille St. Jacques, chicken Walewski, and other postgraduate specialties. Reasonable.

PIONEER HOTEL, Woodside Road, ULmar 1-1896. Open daily for breakfast (from 10 A.M.), lunch (from noon), and dinner (from about 5 P.M.). Bar. Look for the "Woodside" sign in Redwood City, and follow the winding road into a fairly wildsy-woodsy area where some of our Best People have hideaway estates. The Pioneer Hotel is just about as old as its phone number would indicate, and the food is varied (Cornish game hen, squab, veal, scaloppini, etc.). Dancing Wednesday through Saturday. Moderate to fairly expensive.

RICKEY'S RESTAURANT AND STUDIO INN HOTEL, 4219 El Camino Real, Palo Alto, DAvenport 5-3231. Open daily from 7:30 A.M. to midnight for breakfast, lunch, dinner. Bar. If you're a smörgåsbord fancier, Mr. Rickey has as generous a smörgåsbord as you've seen in a month of smörgs. Dinner prices start low and climb steadily.

SCOTTY CAMPBELL'S, 2907 El Camino Real, Atherton, EMerson 6-6762. Open daily except Wednesday from 5:30 P.M. till the last customer hits the road, or the bartender. Scotty Campbell and his wife, Jean, are an attractive pair, and their following is large, loyal, and well fed. Steaks are the specialty here, and the salads are generous too. Your tab will run middling high but you won't leave hungry.

The Campbells, a busy couple, also operate the STEIN ROOM, a handsomely appointed restaurant on El Camino Real in Atherton (open Monday through Friday for lunch from 11:30 A.M. to 2:30 P.M. for men only, for dinner Monday through Saturday from 5 to 10:30 P.M.) and the PLAID PIPER on El Camino Real in Hillsdale (open daily except Sunday for lunch from 11:30 A.M. to 2:30 P.M., for dinner from 5 to 10:30 P.M.). Both places have the Campbell touch

—high quality, large portions, excellent beef—and prices ranging from medium to expensive.

VILLA CHARTIER, 4060 El Camino Real, San Mateo, FIreside 1-3456. Open daily from noon to 10 P.M. for lunch and dinner. Bar. Peninsula ladies in flowery hats twitter like birds all over this attractive place, but there's nothing birdlike about their appetites; the big favorite here is extra-large slabs of roast beef and one of those familiar green salads with a "secret" dressing. Villa Chartier is not dirt cheap, but does a land-office business nonetheless. Next door, and under the same management, is THE LANAI, a Chinese-Polynesian bower where the vegetation is thick, the lights are low, the rum drinks are tall, and the prices are as high as an elephant's thigh.

In Closing

GEORGE STERLING   "The cool, grey city of love."

San Francisco is a city that has inspired a host of adjectives—gay, colorful, charming, cosmopolitan, and so on—but to me there is one that applies more strongly than all the rest.

To me San Francisco is a city of romance. I don't mean the romance of boy meets girl, although this happy phenomenon flourishes splendidly here. I mean the romance of being in a city where a hint of adventure hangs tantalizingly in the cool air. Where a pale yellow light glowing at the end of a dark Chinatown alley can create a sudden feeling of mystery. Where a turn of a corner may bring you face to face with an unexpected vista that makes you stop and stare.

There is romance in a cable-car ride, over the hills and far away, with the city teeming at your very toes. Romance at Top o' the Mark at sunset, with the view more intoxicating than the drink in your hand. Romance in a little North Beach

Lotta's Fountain and the Hearst Building .. San Francisco

restaurant, with a candle glowing on your table and the wine encouraging you to call the waiter "Mario," as all the other customers are doing.

There is romance in the mighty bridges that "couldn't be built," and in the ageless Bay that brought the pioneers and the gold-seekers to the shores of an almost unknown village. And there is romance in the fog that slithers through the Golden Gate and creeps up the hills, drowning the neon lights and mantling the city with its gray majesty.

Romance awaits the traveler in almost every corner of Baghdad-by-the-Bay. I hope you find it, so you can understand why we who live in San Francisco love San Francisco.

Index

219

Index

Index

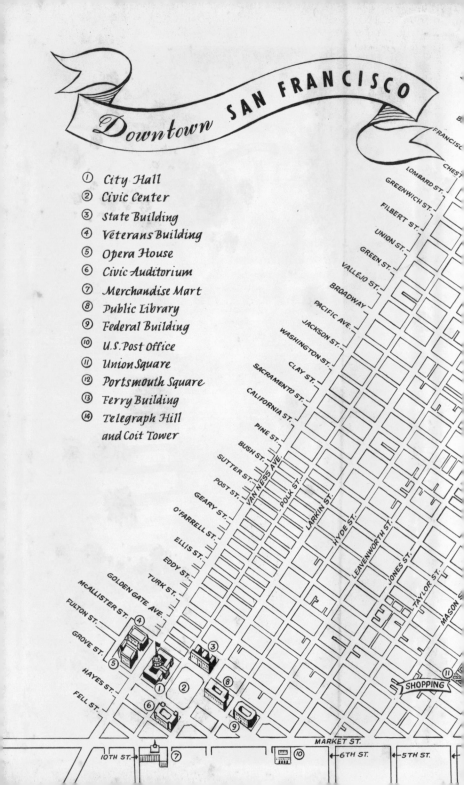